Back *to* Basics

PSYCHOLOGY

A Crash Course for People on the Go

STERLING INNOVATION

New York

STERLING INNOVATION
New York

An Imprint of Sterling Publishing
387 Park Avenue South
New York, NY 10016

Cover art © Seamartini Graphics /Shutterstock (head)

ISBN 978-1-4351-5266-3

This book is part of the *Back to Basics: Psychology* kit and is not to be sold separately.

For information about custom editions, special sales, and premium and
corporate purchases, please contact Sterling Special Sales at 800-805-5489
or specialsales@sterlingpublishing.com.

Manufactured in China

2 4 6 8 10 9 7 5 3 1

www.sterlingpublishing.com

CONTENTS

INTRODUCTION

Psychology is essentially the study of behavior. Behavior is rooted in many cognitive and physiological processes, and psychologists aim to understand these processes in order to solve real-world problems and make sense of our feelings and actions. Almost every aspect of the humanities and the sciences influences psychology in some way, and an understanding of psychology can be valuable in virtually any field, including business, medicine, law, education, and the arts.

Five Main Perspectives

All psychologists share a foundation of knowledge that is rooted in the work of early psychologists, such as Freud, Piaget, and Erikson. They also share a commitment to upholding ethical standards in their research as well as a belief in the scientific approach. However, psychologists may differ from one another in the kinds of questions they ask and how they view the data they find. Therefore, psychology can be divided into roughly five main perspectives.

Biological Psychology

Biological psychologists are interested in the relationship between the body and the mind. They study the structure of the brain and the central nervous system, the parts of the brain and their specific functions, and the links between physical and emotional reactions to events. Biological psychology also focuses on biological processes such as hunger, thirst, and fatigue.

Learning Psychology

Learning is generally defined as a long-lasting change in the way a person or an animal acts or thinks that is attributable to experience. One of the most important concepts in learning psychology is conditioning, which is the way people associate events and outcomes.

Sociocultural Psychology

Sociocultural psychology concerns the ways that the social environment and cultural beliefs shape our lives. Other people, cultural norms, and societal expectations all play a large role in how we act and think and what we consider "normal." Sociocultural psychologists study all aspects of society and culture, including authority, group dynamics, religious beliefs, gender roles and stereotypes, and the day-to-day things, such as food and work, that make up our lives.

Cognitive Psychology

Cognitive psychology is the study of memory, perception, thought, and other mental processes. Cognitive psychologists are concerned with people's emotions, intelligence, motivations, and problem-solving skills. Any subject connected to knowledge, intellect, or the mind in general can fall into the realm of cognitive psychology.

Psychodynamic Psychology

Psychodynamic psychology is the study of unconscious desires and motives, those ideas and feelings that seem to motivate our actions without our being aware of it, including inner conflicts, instincts, and early memories.

Types of Psychologists

Psychologists practice and study psychology in many different ways, though all psychologists generally focus on research, practice, teaching, or a combination of the three. A Ph.D. is not required for many psychology careers, though many psychologists obtain one.

- **Clinical and counseling psychologists** work with adults or children either individually or in groups to help them deal with problems such as depression, anxiety, relationship troubles, or major mental illnesses.
- **Cognitive psychologists** are mostly interested in learning about perception, language, learning, and decision making. Conducting research is often their primary work.
- **Developmental psychologists** are sometimes described as studying people "womb to tomb." They are interested in how people develop, grow, or change throughout the entire life span, from prenatal development to death.
- **Experimental psychologists** are deeply involved in scientific investigation and spend their careers gathering data about different psychological phenomena. Many experimental psychologists specialize in one particular area of research.
- **Industrial-organizational (I/O) psychologists** usually practice in the workplace and are concerned with employee productivity, management, hiring, and quality-of-life issues at work.
- **Neuropsychologists** study brain function. They are concerned with brain-behavior relationships, normal brain functioning, and the effects of accident or illness on the brain.
- **Quantitative psychologists** are experts in all of the methods and statistics of psychological research. They design and evaluate tests, experiments, and other psychological data.

*   *   *

This is by no means a comprehensive list of psychology occupations. Psychologists are employed in virtually every industry, and the study of psychology is not only the application of the scientific method to the investigation of problems but also a philosophy for understanding life itself.

CHAPTER 1:
Development

Life is a series of changes. Beginning as tiny, two-celled organisms, people eventually become babies, children, teenagers, and adults. Countless new skills, both simple and complicated, accompany each new stage. Babies learn how to smile and laugh, children learn how to count and spell, and college students learn how to set their own schedules and wash their own clothes.

All the changes that mark our lives make up a process called development, which is the series of age-related changes that happen over the course of a life span. Many factors influence development, including genes, parental upbringing, parents' educational and economic backgrounds, and life experiences. Even historical events over which we have no control can influence our development.

Theories of Development

Development is the series of age-related changes that happen over the course of a life span. Several famous psychologists, including **Sigmund Freud, Erik Erikson, Jean Piaget**, and **Lawrence Kohlberg**, describe development as a series of stages. A stage is a period in development in which people exhibit typical behavior patterns and establish particular capacities. The various stage theories share three assumptions:

1. People pass through stages in a specific order, with each stage building on capacities developed in the previous stage.
2. Stages are related to age.
3. Development is discontinuous, with qualitatively different capacities emerging in each stage.

Sigmund Freud's Theory of Personality

The Austrian psychiatrist Sigmund Freud first described personality development as a series of stages. Of these stages, Freud believed that early childhood was the most important. He believed that personality developed by about the age of five.

Erik Erikson's Theory of Psychosocial Development

Like Freud, Erik Erikson believed in the importance of early childhood. However, Erikson believed that personality development happens over the entire course of a person's life. In the early 1960s, Erikson proposed a theory that describes eight distinct stages of development. According to Erikson, in each stage people face new challenges, and the stage's outcome depends on how people handle these challenges. Erikson named the stages according to these possible outcomes:

STAGE 1: Trust vs. Mistrust

In the first year after birth, babies depend completely on adults for basic needs such as food, comfort, and warmth. If the caretakers meet these needs reliably, the babies become attached and develop a sense of security. Otherwise, they may develop a mistrustful, insecure attitude.

STAGE 2: Autonomy vs. Shame and Doubt

Between the ages of one and three, toddlers start to gain independence and learn skills such as toilet training, feeding themselves, and dressing themselves. Depending on how they face these challenges, toddlers can develop a sense of autonomy or a sense of doubt and shame about themselves.

STAGE 3: Initiative vs. Guilt

Between the ages of three and six, children must learn to control their impulses and act in a socially responsible way. If they can do this effectively, they become more self-confident. If not, they may develop a strong sense of guilt.

STAGE 4: Industry vs. Inferiority

Between the ages of six and twelve, children compete with peers in school and prepare to take on adult roles. They end this stage with either a sense of competence or a sense of inferiority.

STAGE 5: Identity vs. Role Confusion

During adolescence, which is the period between puberty and adulthood, children try to determine their identity and their direction in life. Depending on their success, they either acquire a sense of identity or remain uncertain about their roles in life.

STAGE 6: Intimacy vs. Isolation

In young adulthood, people face the challenge of developing intimate relationships with others. If they do not succeed, they may become isolated and lonely.

STAGE 7: Generativity vs. Self-Absorption

As people reach middle adulthood, they work to become productive members of society, either through parenting or through their jobs. If they fail, they become overly self-absorbed.

STAGE 8: Integrity vs. Despair

In old age, people examine their lives. They may either have a sense of contentment or be disappointed about their lives and fearful of the future.

Piaget's Theory of Cognitive Development

While conducting intelligence tests on children, Swiss psychologist Jean Piaget began to investigate how children think. According to Piaget, children's thought processes change as they mature physically and interact with the world around them. Piaget believed children develop **schema**, or mental models, to represent the world. As children learn, they expand and modify their schema through the processes of assimilation and accommodation. **Assimilation** is the broadening of an existing schema to include new information. **Accommodation** is the modification of a schema as new information is incorporated.

STAGE 1: Sensorimotor Period

In this stage, which lasts from birth to roughly two years, children learn by using their senses and moving around. By the end of the sensorimotor period, children become capable of **symbolic thought**, which means they can represent objects in terms of mental symbols. More important, children achieve **object permanence** in this stage. Object permanence is the ability to recognize that an object can exist even when it's no longer in one's sight.

STAGE 2: Preoperational Period

This stage lasts from about two to seven years of age. During this stage, children get better at symbolic thought, but they can't yet reason. According to Piaget, children aren't capable of conservation during this stage. **Conservation** is the ability to recognize that measurable physical features of objects, such as length, area, and volume, can be the same even when objects appear different.

STAGE 3: Concrete Operational Period

From the age of seven to about eleven, children become capable of performing mental operations or working through problems and ideas in their minds. However, they can perform operations only on tangible objects and real events. Children also achieve conservation, reversibility, and decentration during this stage:

Reversibility is the ability to mentally reverse actions.
Decentration is the ability to focus simultaneously on several aspects of a problem.

STAGE 4: Formal Operational Period

In this stage, which begins around eleven years of age and continues through adulthood, children become capable of applying mental operations to abstract concepts. They can imagine and reason about hypothetical situations. From this point on, people start to think in abstract, systematic, and logical ways.

Kohlberg's Theory of Moral Development

Lawrence Kohlberg focused on **moral reasoning**, or why people think the way they do about right and wrong. Influenced by Piaget, who believed that moral reasoning depends on the level of cognitive development, Kohlberg proposed that people pass through three levels of moral development. He divided each level into two stages.

LEVEL 1: The Preconventional Level

At this level, children ascribe great importance to the authority of adults. For children in the first stage of this level, an action is wrong if it's punished, whereas in the second stage, an action is right if it's rewarded.

LEVEL 2: The Conventional Level

In the next level, children value rules, which they follow in order to get approval from others. In the first stage of this level, children want the approval only of people who are close to them. In the second stage, children become more concerned with the rules of the broader society.

LEVEL 3: The Postconventional Level

In the final level, people become more flexible and consider what's personally important to them. In the first stage of this level, people still want to follow society's rules, but they don't see those rules as absolute. In the second stage, people figure out right and wrong for themselves, based on abstract ethical principles. Only a small proportion of people reach this last stage of moral reasoning.

Summary

Theories of Development

- Many psychologists have proposed stage theories of development, which argue that people pass through stages in specific orders, with challenges related to age and different capacities emerging in each stage.

- Sigmund Freud first described personality development in terms of stages and believed personality developed by age five.

- Erik Erikson proposed a theory of psychosocial development that occurs in eight stages over a person's lifetime. He proposed that people face new challenges at each stage: trust vs. mistrust, autonomy vs. shame and doubt, initiative vs. guilt, industry vs. inferiority, identity vs. role confusion, intimacy vs. isolation, generativity vs. self-absorption, and integrity vs. despair.

- Jean Piaget's theory of cognitive development states that children develop schema or mental models to represent the world. He proposed four stages of cognitive development: the sensorimotor period, the preoperational period, the concrete operational period, and the formal operational period.

- Lawrence Kohlberg proposed a theory of moral development that includes three levels or stages: the preconventional level, the conventional level, and the postconventional level.

CHAPTER 2:
States of Consciousness

When we sunbathe on a warm day, we notice sensations outside our body, such as the sun shining down, as well as sensations within our body, such as relaxed muscles. Beyond this basic awareness, we are also conscious of ourselves having these experiences. Psychologists define consciousness as the awareness we have of ourselves and our environment.

Consciousness is not static: experiences constantly move in and out of our awareness as our states of mind and environments change. If we fall asleep while sunbathing, we may dream and experience thoughts, feelings, and unconscious desires that aren't always present in our waking state. Drugs and alcohol can also alter consciousness. Alcohol makes us less conscious of our physical sensations and less inhibited, and drugs such as LSD can alter consciousness even more dramatically. Our level of consciousness is, in many ways, both within and out of our control.

Consciousness

Consciousness is the awareness we have of ourselves and our environment. Different states of consciousness are associated with different patterns of brain waves. Brain waves are tracings of electrical activity that is going on in the brain. Scientists record brain waves using an electroencephalograph (EEG), which monitors electrical activity through electrodes placed on the scalp.

Sleep

Sleep is just one of many types of consciousness we experience, and sleep itself comprises several states of consciousness.

Sleep Stages

During one night's sleep, people pass through several cycles of sleep, each lasting about ninety to one hundred minutes. There are five distinct stages of sleep in each cycle: 1, 2, 3, 4, and REM (rapid eye movement).

Stages 1–4

When people fall asleep, they enter into stage 1 sleep, which lasts just a few minutes. Heart rate, breathing rate, and body temperature drop, and muscles relax. Fantasies or bizarre images may float around in the mind.

After a few minutes of stage 1 sleep, people move into stage 2 sleep. Stage 2 lasts about twenty minutes and is characterized by short bursts of brain waves called **sleep spindles**. People then pass into slow-wave sleep, which occurs during stages 3 and 4. People in stage 3 and 4 sleep show slow breathing and pulse rates, have limp muscles, and are difficult to rouse.

REM Sleep

At the end of stage 4, people go back through the stages in reverse, from stage 4 to 3 to 2 to 1. When they reach stage 1, instead of waking up, people go into REM sleep.

REM sleep is a stage of deep sleep in which, paradoxically, brain wave activity resembles that of an alert person. During REM sleep, pulse rate and breathing become irregular, eyes move rapidly under closed lids, and muscles remain very relaxed. Genital arousal also happens during REM. In women, the clitoris becomes swollen with blood, and vaginal lubrication increases. In men, the penis becomes erect. Although dreaming happens in other sleep stages as well, dreams are most vivid and frequent during REM sleep.

Dreams

The function of dreams is as much a mystery as the function of sleep.

Freud's Dream Theory

Psychoanalyst **Sigmund Freud** believed that dreams allow people to express unconscious wishes they find unacceptable in real life. He drew a distinction between the **manifest content** and the **latent content** of dreams. The manifest content is the plot of the dream: who's in the dream, what happens, and so on. The latent content is the dream's hidden meaning. According to Freud, the manifest content is a symbolic representation of the latent content.

Activation-Synthesis Theory

Another theory, called the **activation-synthesis theory**, proposes that neurons in the brain randomly activate during REM sleep. Dreams arise when the cortex of the brain tries to make meaning out of these random neural impulses.

Problem-Solving Dreams

Some researchers think that dreams express people's most pressing concerns and might help to solve problems in day-to-day life. If someone has an important job interview coming up, for example, he may rehearse scenarios for the interview in his dreams.

Neural Housekeeping

Some theories argue that dreams arise during the brain's routine housekeeping functions, such as eliminating or strengthening neural connections. Dreams, then, are a way of cleaning up brain files.

During **lucid dreams**, people are aware that they are dreaming and may be able to control their actions to some extent within the dream.

Altered States

Some states of consciousness don't occur naturally and must be induced in some way. These include hypnotic states, meditative states, and drug-induced states.

Hypnosis

Hypnosis is a procedure that opens people to the power of suggestion. A hypnotist puts a subject in an altered state by encouraging relaxation and sleepiness and often describing the sorts of physical sensations a subject should be feeling. Once a subject is in the altered state, he or she may act, perceive, think, or feel according to the hypnotist's suggestions. Not everyone can be hypnotized, and some people are more hypnotizable than others.

A hypnotic state isn't sleep—brain waves, for example, do not reliably change during hypnosis as they do during sleep. Researchers don't even agree that hypnosis is an altered state of consciousness. Researchers propose two main theories about hypnosis:

- **Ernest Hilgard** proposed that hypnosis causes people to dissociate or divide their consciousness into two parts. One part responds to the outside world, and the other part observes but doesn't participate. According to this theory, hypnosis can make people not react to pain because hypnosis separates the part of consciousness that registers pain from the part of consciousness that communicates with the outside world.
- Many other researchers, such as Theodore Barber and Nicholas Spanos, think hypnosis happens when a suggestible person plays the role of a hypnotized person. According to this theory, hypnotized people simply behave as they think they are expected to.

Meditation

Meditation is the practice of focusing attention. People meditate to enhance awareness and gain more control of physical and mental processes. Techniques used in meditation vary and include activities such as repetitive chanting and breathing exercises.

Meditative states are associated with an increase in alpha and theta brain waves, and physical indicators of relaxation such as slowed pulse and breathing. Some researchers have found that meditation has long-term effects such as improving physical and mental health and reducing stress. However, researchers disagree about whether meditative states are unique states of consciousness. Some researchers believe relaxation techniques can produce the same kind of state produced by meditation.

Psychoactive Drugs

Psychoactive drugs, as opposed to medicinal drugs, have psychological effects, meaning that they change sensory experience, perception, mood, thinking, and behavior. Psychoactive drugs are sometimes called recreational drugs, though some have legitimate medical uses.

Types of Recreational Drugs

Researchers usually classify recreational drugs into four types:

- **Stimulants:** drugs that stimulate the central nervous system
- **Sedatives:** drugs that slow down the central nervous system
- **Narcotics:** also called opiates; drugs that can relieve pain
- **Hallucinogens:** drugs that cause sensory and perceptual distortions

Drugs derived from the cannabis plant, such as marijuana and hashish, have features of more than one of these drug types, so researchers sometimes consider cannabis to be a separate, fifth drug type.

How Psychoactive Drugs Work

Psychoactive drugs work by affecting neurotransmitter function. A single drug can affect the function of more than one neurotransmitter. Drugs can:

- Cause more or less of a neurotransmitter to be released at synapses
- Block reuptake of a neurotransmitter by presynaptic cells
- Stimulate or block neurotransmitter receptors on postsynaptic cells

Influences on Psychoactive Drug Effects

A given drug doesn't always have the same effect. If ten people drink beer one evening, they all may have different experiences. The effect of a drug depends on many different factors:

- The amount of the drug
- The potency of the drug
- How the drug is administered
- How much previous experience a user has with the drug
- The user's age and body weight
- The user's mood, personality, and motivation
- The environment in which the drug is used
- The user's expectations about the drug's effects

Chronic Use of Psychoactive Drugs

When people regularly use a drug, they may develop a tolerance to it. As time goes on, people with a **tolerance** need more and more of the drug to get the same effect.

When people stop using a drug after a long period of regular use, they often experience **withdrawal symptoms**. Different drugs produce different kinds of withdrawal symptoms. Not all drugs are addictive.

With chronic use, people can get physically or psychologically dependent on a drug. **Physical dependence** happens when a person must take the drug to avoid withdrawal symptoms.

Psychological dependence is when a person keeps taking the drug because of cravings. A drug can be both physically and psychologically addictive.

Drug use can be dangerous for several reasons. Heavy or frequent use of drugs can damage body tissues and organs. Overdoses of some drugs, including sedatives, stimulants, and narcotics, can be lethal. Drugs can have dangerous indirect effects by causing people to behave in risky, accident-prone, or unhealthy ways.

Summary

Consciousness
- Consciousness is the awareness people have of themselves and the environment around them.
- The level and state of consciousness vary. Different states of consciousness are associated with different brain wave patterns. Brain waves are tracings that show the kind of electrical activity going on in the brain. Scientists use an electroencephalograph, or EEG, to record these waves.

Sleep
- There are five stages of sleep. At each stage, different types of brain waves function, and heart rate, breathing, and temperature vary.
- During REM sleep, heart rate and breathing become irregular, eyes move rapidly, and muscles relax. Dreams are most vivid during REM sleep.

Dreams
- Sigmund Freud believed that dreams allow people to express unconscious wishes. He said the manifest content of dreams, or the dream's plot, symbolizes the latent content, or hidden meaning.
- The activation-synthesis theory proposes that neurons in the brain randomly activate during REM sleep. Dreams arise when the cortex tries to make sense of these impulses.
- Some researchers think dreams express people's most pressing concerns, while others think dreams arise during the brain's routine housekeeping chores such as eliminating or strengthening neural connections.

Altered States

- Altered states are induced states of consciousness and include hypnotic states, meditative states, and drug-induced states.
- In hypnosis, a hypnotist makes suggestions to a person. One theory states that people in hypnosis divide their consciousness into two parts. Other theories say that people merely play a role when hypnotized.
- Meditation is the practice of focusing attention.
- Psychoactive drugs are usually used for recreational rather than medical purposes, though some have legitimate medical uses. These drugs change sensory experience, perception, mood, thinking, and behavior.
- Recreational drugs include stimulants, sedatives, narcotics, and hallucinogens.
- Drugs work by affecting neurotransmitter function in various ways.
- The effect of any drug depends on many factors such as the amount of the drug, how the drug is administered, and the user's mood, personality, and motivation.
- Chronic use of drugs can result in tolerance, withdrawal symptoms, physical dependence, or psychological dependence.
- Drug use can be dangerous.

CHAPTER 3:
Learning and Conditioning

A vast amount of time and effort is spent on the business of learning, and any teacher or student will agree that learning is not always a simple matter. If a teacher tells a child to stay away from kids on the swings, the child may not always remember and obey—until a few collisions teach him his lesson. A kindergartener may need to watch her father tie his shoes dozens of times before she understands how to do it herself. Psychologists define learning as a change in behavior or knowledge that results from experience.

Three kinds of learning are of particular importance to psychologists. Classical conditioning is learning that depends on associations between events, such as learning to walk far from the swings to avoid collisions. Operant conditioning is learning that depends on the consequences of behavior, such as learning that getting a good night's sleep before an exam will help to earn a good grade. Observational learning involves learning by watching others, such as learning to tie shoelaces by watching someone else do it first.

Classical Conditioning

Russian physiologist **Ivan Pavlov** was the first to describe **classical conditioning**. In classical conditioning, also called respondent conditioning or Pavlovian conditioning, a subject comes to respond to a neutral stimulus as he would to another, non-neutral stimulus by learning to associate the two stimuli.

Pavlov's contribution to learning began with his study of dogs. Not surprisingly, his dogs drooled every time he gave them food. Then he noticed that if he sounded a tone every time he fed them, the dogs soon started to drool at the sound of the tone, even if no food followed it. The dogs had come to associate the tone, a neutral stimulus, with food, a non-neutral stimulus.

Conditioned and Unconditioned Stimuli and Responses

Psychologists use several terms to talk about classical conditioning. In Pavlov's experiment, salivation was the **unconditioned response**, which is a response that occurs naturally. Food was the **unconditioned stimulus**, the stimulus that naturally evoked salivation. The tone was the **conditioned stimulus**, the stimulus that the dogs learned to associate with food. The **conditioned response** to the tone was salivation. The conditioned response is usually the same as, or similar to, the unconditioned response.

Operant Conditioning

In the late nineteenth century, psychologist **Edward Thorndike** proposed the law of effect. The **law of effect** states that any behavior that has good consequences will tend to be repeated, and any behavior that has bad consequences will tend to be avoided. In the 1930s, another psychologist, **B. F. Skinner**, extended this idea and began to study operant conditioning. **Operant conditioning** is a type of learning in which responses come to be controlled by their consequences. Operant responses are often new responses.

Skinner used a device called the Skinner box to study operant conditioning. A **Skinner box** is a cage set up so that an animal can automatically get a food reward if it makes a particular kind of response. The box also contains an instrument that records the number of responses an animal makes. Psychologists use several key terms to discuss operant conditioning principles, including *reinforcement* and *punishment*.

Reinforcement

Reinforcement is delivery of a consequence that increases the likelihood that a response will occur. **Positive reinforcement** is the presentation of a stimulus after a response so that the response will occur more often. **Negative reinforcement** is the removal of a stimulus after a response so that the response will occur more often. In this terminology, *positive* and *negative* don't mean good and bad. Instead, *positive* means adding a stimulus, and *negative* means removing a stimulus.

Punishment

Punishment is the delivery of a consequence that decreases the likelihood that a response will occur. Positive and negative punishments are analogous to positive and negative reinforcement. **Positive punishment** is the presentation of a stimulus after a response so that the response will occur less often. **Negative punishment** is the removal of a stimulus after a response so that the response will occur less often.

Reinforcement helps to increase a behavior, while punishment helps to decrease a behavior.

Shaping

Shaping is a procedure in which reinforcement is used to guide a response closer and closer to a desired response.

Reinforcement Schedules

A **reinforcement schedule** is the pattern in which reinforcement is given over time. Reinforcement schedules can be continuous or intermittent. In **continuous reinforcement**, someone provides reinforcement every time a particular response occurs. In **intermittent** or **partial reinforcement**, someone provides reinforcement on only some of the occasions on which the response occurs.

Biological Influences

Conditioning accounts for a lot of learning, both in humans and nonhuman species. However, biological factors can limit the capacity for conditioning. Two good examples of biological influences on conditioning are taste aversion and instinctive drift.

Taste Aversion

Psychologist John Garcia and his colleagues found that aversion to a particular taste is conditioned only by pairing the taste (a conditioned stimulus) with nausea (an unconditioned stimulus). If taste is paired with other unconditioned stimuli, conditioning doesn't occur.

Similarly, nausea paired with most other conditioned stimuli doesn't produce aversion to those stimuli. Pairing taste and nausea, on the other hand, produces conditioning very quickly, even with a delay of several hours between the conditioned stimulus of the taste and the unconditioned stimulus of nausea. This phenomenon is unusual, since normally classical conditioning occurs only when the unconditioned stimulus immediately follows the conditioned stimulus.

Instinctive Drift

Instinctive drift is the tendency for conditioning to be hindered by natural instincts. Two psychologists, Keller and Marian Breland, were the first to describe instinctive drift. The Brelands found that through operant conditioning, they could teach raccoons to put a coin in a box by using food as a reinforcer. However, they couldn't teach raccoons to put two coins in a box. If given two coins, raccoons just held on to the coins and rubbed them together. Giving the raccoons two coins brought out their instinctive food-washing behavior: raccoons instinctively rub edible things together to clean them before eating them. Once the coins became associated with food, it became impossible to train them to drop the coins into the box.

Cognitive Influences

Researchers once thought of conditioning as automatic and not involving much in the way of higher mental processes. However, now researchers believe that conditioning does involve some information processing.

The psychologist **Robert Rescorla** showed that in classical conditioning, pairing two stimuli doesn't always produce the same level of conditioning. Conditioning works better if the conditioned stimulus acts as a reliable signal that predicts the appearance of the unconditioned stimulus.

The fact that classical conditioning depends on the predictive power of the conditioned stimulus, rather than just association of two stimuli, means that some information processing happens during classical conditioning. Cognitive processes are also involved in operant conditioning. A response doesn't increase just because satisfying consequences follow the response. People usually think about whether the response caused the consequence. If the response did cause the consequence, then it makes sense to keep responding the same way. Otherwise, it doesn't.

Observational Learning

People and animals also learn by observing others. **Observational learning** is the process of learning to respond in a particular way by watching others, who are called models. Observational learning is also called vicarious conditioning because it involves learning by watching others acquire responses through classical or operant conditioning.

The person best know for research on observational learning is psychologist Albert Bandura, who did some landmark experiments showing that children who watched adults behaving aggressively were more likely to behave aggressively themselves. In the experiment, Bandura let a group of kindergarteners watch a film of an adult violently attacking an inflatable plastic toy shaped like Bobo the clown by hitting it, sitting on it, hammering it, and so forth. He then let the children into a room with Bobo dolls. The children precisely imitated the adult's behavior, gleefully attacking Bobo. Their behavior was a type of observational learning.

Summary

Classical Conditioning

- Ivan Pavlov was the first to describe classical conditioning, the type of learning in which a subject comes to respond to a neutral stimulus as he would to another stimulus by learning to associate the two stimuli.
- An unconditioned response is the naturally occurring response; an unconditioned stimulus is the stimulus that evokes an innate response.
- A conditioned response is the learned response; a conditioned stimulus is the learned or associated stimulus.
- A conditioned response is acquired when a conditioned stimulus is paired with an unconditioned stimulus.

Operant Conditioning

- Operant conditioning is a type of learning in which responses come to be controlled by their consequences.
- B. F. Skinner used a device called a Skinner box to study operant conditioning in rats. He set up the boxes so that the rats could automatically get rewards or punishments for particular types of responses.
- Reinforcement is delivery of a consequence that increases the likelihood that a response will occur. Positive reinforcement is the presentation of a stimulus after a response. Negative reinforcement is the removal of a stimulus after a response.
- Punishment is the delivery of a consequence that decreases the likelihood that a response will occur. Positive punishment is the

presentation of a stimulus after a response. Negative punishment is the removal of a stimulus after a response.

- Shaping is a procedure in which reinforcement is used to guide a response closer and closer to a desired response.

Biological Influences

- Biological factors can limit conditioning.
- Aversion to a particular taste can be conditioned only by pairing the taste with nausea.
- *Instinctive drift* is the tendency for conditioning to be hindered by natural instincts.

Cognitive Influences

- Conditioning involves higher mental processes, as it depends on the predictive power of the conditioned stimulus rather than mere association of stimuli.

Observational Learning

- Observational learning is the process of learning to respond in a particular way by watching others, or models.
- Albert Bandura conducted experiments showing that children who watched adults behaving aggressively were more likely to behave aggressively themselves.

CHAPTER 4:
Memory

On a basic level, memory is the capacity for storing and retrieving information, but memories are not simply recorded and neatly stored. Our memories are selected, constructed, and edited not just by us but by the world around us. We have an astounding, boundless capacity for memory, but our memories are also faulty, full of holes and distortions, and hampered by unreliable data-retrieval systems.

Memory researchers explore the many mysteries of remembering. They try to explain why we have trouble remembering a person's name—only to recall it later, after the person is gone. We still have much to learn about how memories are made and what determines whether they last or fade away.

Memory Processes

Memory is essentially the capacity for storing and retrieving information. Three processes are involved in memory: encoding, storage, and retrieval. All three of these processes determine whether something is remembered or forgotten.

Encoding

Processing information into memory is called **encoding**. People automatically encode some types of information without being aware of it. For example, most people probably can recall where they ate lunch yesterday, even though they didn't try to remember this information. However, other types of information become encoded only if people pay attention to it. College students will probably not remember all the material in their textbooks unless they pay close attention while they're reading.

There are several different ways of encoding verbal information:

- Structural encoding focuses on what words look like. For instance, one might note whether words are long or short, in uppercase or lowercase, or handwritten or typed.
- Phonemic encoding focuses on how words sound.
- Semantic encoding focuses on the meaning of words. Semantic encoding requires a deeper level of processing than structural or phonemic encoding and usually results in better memory.

Storage

After information enters the brain, it has to be stored or maintained. To describe the process of storage, many psychologists use the three-stage model proposed by **Richard Atkinson** and **Richard Shiffrin**. According to this model, information is stored sequentially in three memory systems: sensory, short-term, and long-term.

Sensory Memory

Sensory memory stores incoming sensory information in detail but only for an instant. The capacity of sensory memory is very large, but the information in it is unprocessed. If a flashlight moves quickly in a circle inside a dark room, people will see a circle of light rather than the individual points through which the flashlight moved. This happens because sensory memory holds the successive images of the moving flashlight long enough for the brain to see a circle. Visual sensory memory is called **iconic memory**; auditory sensory memory is called **echoic memory**.

Some of the information in sensory memory transfers to **short-term memory**, which can hold information for approximately twenty seconds. Rehearsing can help keep information in short-term memory longer. When people repeat a new phone number over and over to themselves, they are rehearsing it and keeping it in short-term memory.

Short-term memory has a limited capacity: it can store about seven pieces of information, plus or minus two pieces. These pieces of information can be small, such as individual numbers or letters, or larger, such as familiar strings of numbers, words, or sentences. A method called chunking can help to increase the capacity of short-term memory. **Chunking** combines small bits of information into bigger, familiar pieces.

Psychologists today consider short-term memory to be a **working memory**. Rather than being just a temporary information storage system, working memory is an active system. Information can be kept in working memory while people process or examine it. Working memory allows people to temporarily store and manipulate visual images, store information while trying to make decisions, and remember a phone number long enough to write it down.

Information can be transferred from short-term memory to long-term memory and from long-term memory back to short-term memory. **Long-term memory** has an almost infinite capacity, and information in long-term memory usually stays there for the duration of a person's life. However, this doesn't mean that people will always be able to remember what's in their long-term memory—they may not be able to retrieve information that's there.

Organization of Memories

Imagine what would happen if a psychology textbook weren't organized by section, by chapter, or in any other way. If the textbook just contained lots of information in a random order, students would have difficulty finding a particular concept, such as "encoding of memory." They'd know the information was in there somewhere, but they'd have trouble retrieving it.

Long-term memory stores much more information than a textbook, and people would never be able to retrieve the information from it if it weren't organized in some way.

Psychologists believe one way the brain organizes information in long-term memory is by category. For example, *papaya* may be organized within the semantic category *fruit*. Categories can also be based on how words sound or look. If someone is struggling to remember the word *papaya*, she may remember first that it's a three-syllable word, that it begins with the letter *p*, or that it ends with the letter *a*.

Long-term memory organizes information not only by categories but also by the information's familiarity, relevance, or connection to other information.

Retrieval

Retrieval is the process of getting information out of memory. **Retrieval cues** are stimuli that help the process of retrieval. Retrieval cues include associations, context, and mood.

Associations

Because the brain stores information as networks of associated concepts, recalling a particular word becomes easier if another, related word is recalled first. This process is called **priming**.

Context

People can often remember an event by placing themselves in the same context they were in when the event happened.

Mood

If people are in the same mood they were in during an event, they may have an easier time recalling the event.

Types of Memory

Psychologists often make distinctions among different types of memory. There are three main distinctions:

1. Implicit Vs. Explicit Memory

Sometimes information that unconsciously enters the memory affects thoughts and behavior, even though the event and the memory of the event remain unknown. Such unconscious retention of information is called **implicit memory**.

Explicit memory is conscious, intentional remembering of information. Remembering a social security number involves explicit memory.

2. Declarative Vs. Procedural Memory

Declarative memory is recall of factual information such as dates, words, faces, events, and concepts. Remembering the capital of France, the rules for playing football, and what happened in the last game of the World Series involves declarative memory. Declarative memory is usually considered to be explicit because it involves conscious, intentional remembering.

Procedural memory is recall of how to do things such as swimming or driving a car. Procedural memory is usually considered implicit because people don't have to consciously remember how to perform actions or skills.

3. Semantic Vs. Episodic Memory

Declarative memory is of two types: semantic and episodic. **Semantic memory** is recall of general facts, while **episodic memory** is recall of personal facts. Remembering the capital of France and the rules for playing football uses semantic memory. Remembering what happened in the last game of the World Series uses episodic memory.

Forgetting

Memory researchers certainly haven't forgotten **Hermann Ebbinghaus**, the first person to do scientific studies of forgetting, using himself as a subject. He spent a lot of time memorizing endless lists of nonsense syllables and then testing himself to see whether he remembered them. He found that he forgot most of what he learned during the first few hours after learning it.

Later researchers have found that forgetting doesn't always occur that quickly. Meaningful information fades more slowly than nonsense syllables. The rate at which people forget or retain information also depends on what method is used to measure forgetting and retention. **Retention** is the proportion of learned information that is retained or remembered—the flip side of forgetting.

Measures of Forgetting and Retention

Researchers measure forgetting and retention in three different ways: recall, recognition, and relearning.

Recall

Recall is remembering without any external cues. For example, essay questions test recall of knowledge because nothing on a blank sheet of paper will jog the memory.

Recognition is identifying learned information using external cues. For example, true-or-false questions and multiple-choice questions test recognition because the previously learned information is there on the page, along with other options. In general, recognition is easier than recall.

Relearning

When using the **relearning** method to measure retention, a researcher might ask a subject to memorize a long grocery list. She might measure how long he has to practice before he remembers every item. Suppose it takes him ten minutes. On another day, she gives him the same list again and measures how much time he takes to relearn the list. Suppose he now learns it in five minutes. He has saved five minutes of learning time, or 50 percent of the original time it took him to learn it. His savings score of 50 percent indicates that he retained 50 percent of the information he learned the first time.

Causes of Forgetting

There are six main reasons for forgetting: ineffective encoding, decay, interference, retrieval failure, motivated forgetting, and physical injury or trauma.

Ineffective Encoding

The way information is **encoded** affects the ability to remember it. Processing information at a deeper level makes it harder to forget. If a student thinks about the meaning of the concepts in her textbook rather than just reading them, she'll remember them better when the final exam comes around. If the information is not encoded properly—such as if the student simply skims over the textbook while paying more attention to the TV—it is more likely to be forgotten.

Decay

According to **decay theory,** memory fades with time. Decay explains the loss of memories from sensory and short-term memory. However, loss of long-term memories does not seem to depend on how much time has gone by since the information was learned. People might easily remember their first day in junior high school but completely forget what they learned in class last Tuesday.

Interference

Interference theory has a better account of why people lose long-term memories. According to this theory, people forget information because of interference from other learned information.

Retrieval Failure

Forgetting may also result from failure to **retrieve** information in memory, such as if the wrong sort of **retrieval cue** is used. For example, Dan may not be able to remember the name of his fifth-grade teacher. However, the teacher's name might suddenly pop into Dan's head if he visits his old grade school and sees his fifth-grade classroom.

Motivated Forgetting

Psychiatrist **Sigmund Freud** proposed that people forget because they push unpleasant or intolerable thoughts and feelings deep into their unconscious. He called this phenomenon **repression**. The idea that people forget things they don't want to remember is also called **motivated forgetting** or psychogenic amnesia.

Physical Injury or Trauma

Anterograde amnesia is the inability to remember events that occur after an injury or traumatic event. **Retrograde amnesia** is the inability to remember events that occurred before an injury or traumatic event.

The Biology of Memory

Researchers still don't know exactly how memory works at the physiological level. Long-term memory involves the **hippocampus** area of the brain. Some researchers think the hippocampus binds together different elements of a memory, which are stored in separate areas of the brain. In other words, the hippocampus helps with memory organization. Other researchers think that the hippocampus helps with memory **consolidation**, or the transfer of information into long-term memory.

The brain area involved in processing a memory may determine where memories are stored. For example, memories of visual information probably end up in the visual cortex. Research suggests that there may be specific neural circuits for particular memories. Psychologists also think that memory relates to changes in neurotransmitter release from neurons, fluctuations in hormone levels, and protein synthesis in the brain.

Summary

Memory Processes

- The three processes involved in memory are encoding, storage, and retrieval.
- Encoding is putting information into memory and includes structural, phonemic, and semantic encoding.

- In storage, information is maintained in a three-stage process involving sensory memory, short-term memory, and long-term memory.
- Long-term memory is organized into categories, as well as by familiarity, relevance, and relationship to other memories.
- Retrieval is the process of getting information out of memory.
- Retrieval cues are stimuli that help get information out of memory.
- Retrieval cues include associations, context, and mood.

Types of Memory
- Implicit memory is unconscious retaining of information, whereas explicit memory is conscious, intentional remembering.
- Declarative memory is recall of factual information, whereas procedural memory is recall of how to do things.
- Semantic memory is recall of general facts, while episodic memory is recall of personal facts.

Forgetting
- Hermann Ebbinghaus was the first researcher to conduct scientific studies of forgetting. Using himself as a subject, he discovered that much information is forgotten within a few hours after learning it.
- Retention is the proportion of learned information that is remembered.
- Researchers use three methods to measure forgetting and retention: recall, recognition, and relearning.
- Causes of forgetting include ineffective encoding, decay, interference, retrieval failure, and motivated forgetting.

The Biology of Memory
- The hippocampus is involved in long-term memory.
- Memories may be stored in different areas of the brain.
- There may specific neural circuits for particular memories.

CHAPTER 5:
Language and Cognition

Cognitive psychology concerns both language and thought and has been popular only since the 1950s. Before that, many psychologists believed that the scientific method could not be applied toward study of a process as private as thinking. From ancient Greek times, only philosophers and metaphysicians studied the nature of language and thought. The metaphysician René Descartes, for example, famously argued, "I think, therefore I am."

Today, thanks to increasingly sophisticated tools for studying brain activity, cognitive psychology is a thriving science. Cognitive psychologists explore such questions as how language affects thought, whether it is possible to create a "thinking" machine, and why humans are motivated to create art.

The Structure of Language

Language is a system of symbols and rules that is used for meaningful communication. A system of communication has to meet certain criteria in order to be considered a language:

- A language uses **symbols**, which are sounds, gestures, or written characters that represent objects, actions, events, and ideas. Symbols enable people to refer to objects that are in another place or events that occurred at a different time.
- A language is meaningful and therefore can be understood by other users of that language.
- A language is **generative**, which means that the symbols of a language can be combined to produce an infinite number of messages.
- A language has rules that govern how symbols can be arranged. These rules allow people to understand messages in that language even if they have never encountered those messages before.

Theories of Language Acquisition

The nature versus nurture debate extends to the topic of language acquisition. Today, most researchers acknowledge that both nature and nurture play a role in language acquisition. However, some researchers emphasize the influences of learning on language acquisition, while others emphasize the biological influences.

Environmental Influences on Language Acquisition

A major proponent of the idea that language depends largely on environment was the behaviorist **B. F. Skinner**. He believed that language is acquired through principles of conditioning, including association, imitation, and reinforcement.

According to this view, children learn words by associating sounds with objects, actions, and events. They also learn words and syntax by imitating others. Adults enable children to learn words and syntax by reinforcing correct speech.

Biological Influences on Language Acquisition

The main proponent of the view that biological influences bring about language development is the well-known linguist **Noam Chomsky**. Chomsky argues that human brains have a language acquisition device (LAD), an innate mechanism or process that allows children to develop language skills. According to this view, all children are born with a universal grammar, which makes them receptive to the common features of all languages. Because of this hard-wired background in grammar, children easily pick up a language when they are exposed to its particular grammar.

Evidence for an innate human capacity to acquire language skills comes from the following observations:

- The stages of language development occur at about the same ages in most children, even though different children experience very different environments.

- Children's language development follows a similar pattern across cultures.
- Children generally acquire language skills quickly and effortlessly.
- Deaf children who have not been exposed to a language may make up their own language. These new languages resemble each other in sentence structure, even when they are created in different cultures.

The Structure of Cognition

Cognition, or thinking, involves mental activities such as understanding, problem solving, and decision making. Cognition also makes creativity possible.

The Building Blocks of Cognition

When humans think, they manipulate mental representations of objects, actions, events, and ideas. Humans commonly use mental representations such as concepts, prototypes, and cognitive schemas.

- A **concept** is a mental category that groups similar objects, events, qualities, or actions. Concepts summarize information, enabling humans to think quickly.
- A **prototype** is a typical example of a concept. Humans use prototypes to decide whether a particular instance of something belongs to a concept.
- **Cognitive schemas** are mental models of different aspects of the world. They contain knowledge, beliefs, assumptions, associations, and expectations.

Theories of Cognitive Development

Cognitive development refers to the change in children's patterns of thinking as they grow older.

Jean Piaget's Stage Theory

The scientist best known for research on cognitive development is **Jean Piaget,** who proposed that children's thinking goes through a set series of four major stages. Piaget believed that children's cognitive skills unfold naturally as they mature and explore their environment.

Lev Vygotsky's Theory of Sociocultural Influences

Psychologist **Lev Vygotsky** believed that children's sociocultural environment plays an important role in how they develop cognitively. In Vygotsky's view, the acquisition of language is a crucial part of cognitive development. After children acquire language, they don't just go through a set series of stages. Rather, their cognitive development depends on interactions with adults, cultural norms, and their environmental circumstances.

Current Research on Cognitive Development

Current research indicates that children have complex cognitive abilities at much younger ages than Piaget suggested. For example, a four-month-old infant can recognize that solid objects cannot pass through other solid objects and that objects roll down slopes instead of rolling up. At five months of age, infants can recognize the correct answers to addition and subtraction problems involving small numbers. These observations have led some researchers to speculate that humans are born with some basic cognitive abilities.

Critics argue that researchers who find these results are overinterpreting the behavior of the infants they study.

Creativity

Creativity is the ability to generate novel, valuable ideas. People need a minimum level of intelligence to be creative, but not all people who get high scores on intelligence tests are creative.

Divergent vs. Convergent Thinking

Creativity is characterized by **divergent thinking**. In divergent thinking, people's thoughts go off in different directions as they try to generate many different solutions to a problem.

In **convergent thinking**, on the other hand, people narrow down a list of possibilities to arrive at a single right answer.

Characteristics of Creative People

Researchers have identified several characteristics that creative people share:

- **Expertise:** Creative people usually have considerable training, knowledge, and expertise in their field.
- **Nonconformity:** Creative people tend to think independently and have relatively little concern for what others think of them.
- **Curiosity:** Creative people tend to be open to new experiences and willing to explore unusual events.
- **Persistence:** Creative people are usually willing to work hard to overcome obstacles and take risks.
- **Intrinsic motivation:** Creative people tend to be motivated more by intrinsic rewards, such as a sense of accomplishment or satisfaction of curiosity, rather than by extrinsic rewards, such as money or social approval.

Summary

The Structure of Language

- Language is a system of symbols and rules used for meaningful communication.

Theories of Language Acquisition

- Behaviorist B. F. Skinner believed that language depends largely on environment and that people acquire language through principles of conditioning.

- Critics argue the inadequacy of behaviorist explanations.
- Some cognitive neuroscientists have created neural networks that can acquire some aspects of language by encountering many examples of language. They think children may acquire language in the same way.
- Noam Chomsky proposed that human brains have a language acquisition device that allows children to acquire language easily.

The Structure of Cognition

- Cognition involves activities such as understanding, problem solving, decision making, and being creative.
- People use mental representations such as concepts, prototypes, and cognitive schemas when they think.

Theories of Cognitive Development

- Jean Piaget believed that children's cognitive skills unfold naturally as they mature and explore their environment.
- Lev Vygotsky believed that children's sociocultural environment plays an important role in cognitive development.
- Some researchers have shown that humans are born with some basic cognitive abilities.

Creativity

- Creativity is the ability to generate novel, useful ideas.
- Some characteristics of creative people are expertise, nonconformity, curiosity, persistence, and intrinsic motivation.

CHAPTER 6:
Intelligence

Few people agree on exactly what "intelligence" is or how to measure it. The nature and origin of intelligence are elusive, and the value and accuracy of intelligence tests are often uncertain. Researchers who study intelligence often argue about what IQ tests really measure and whether or not Einstein's theories and Yo Yo Ma's cello playing show different types of intelligence.

Intelligence is a particularly thorny subject since research in the field has the potential to affect many social and political decisions, such as how much funding the U.S. government should devote to educational programs. People who believe that intelligence is mainly inherited don't see the usefulness in special educational opportunities for the underprivileged, while people who believe that environment plays a large role in intelligence tend to support such programs. The importance and effects of intelligence are clear, but intelligence does not lend itself to easy definition or explanation.

Theories of Intelligence

Intelligence includes the ability to benefit from past experience, act purposefully, solve problems, and adapt to new situations. Intelligence can also be defined as "the ability that intelligence tests measure." There is a long history of disagreement about what actually constitutes intelligence.

The G Factor

Charles Spearman proposed a **general intelligence factor**, g, which underlies all intelligent behavior. Many scientists still believe in a general intelligence factor that underlies the specific abilities that intelligence tests measure. Other scientists are skeptical, because people can score high on one specific ability but show weakness in others.

Eight Types of Intelligence

In the 1980s and 1990s, psychologist **Howard Gardner** proposed the idea of not one kind of intelligence but eight, which are relatively independent of one another. These eight types of intelligence are:

1. **Linguistic:** spoken and written language skills
2. **Logical–mathematical:** number skills
3. **Musical:** performance or composition skills
4. **Spatial:** ability to evaluate and analyze the visual world
5. **Bodily-kinesthetic:** dance or athletic abilities
6. **Interpersonal:** skill in understanding and relating to others
7. **Intrapersonal:** skill in understanding the self
8. **Nature:** skill in understanding the natural world

Gardner believes that each of these domains of intelligence has inherent value but that culture and context may cause some domains to be emphasized over others. Critics of the idea of multiple intelligences maintain that these abilities are talents rather than kinds of intelligence.

Triarchic Theory of Intelligence

Also in the 1980s and 1990s, **Robert Sternberg** proposed a **triarchic theory of intelligence** that distinguishes among three aspects of intelligence:

- **Componential intelligence:** the ability assessed by intelligence tests
- **Experiential intelligence:** the ability to adapt to new situations and produce new ideas
- **Contextual intelligence:** the ability to function effectively in daily situations

Emotional Intelligence

Some researchers distinguish **emotional intelligence** as an ability that helps people to perceive, express, understand, and regulate emotions. Other researchers maintain that this ability is a collection of personality traits such as empathy and extroversion, rather than a kind of intelligence.

Intelligence Testing

The **psychometric approach** to intelligence emphasizes people's performance on standardized aptitude tests. **Aptitude tests** predict people's future ability to acquire skills or knowledge. **Achievement tests**, on the other hand, measure skills and knowledge that people have already learned.

Types of Tests

Intelligence tests can be given individually or to groups of people. The best-known individual intelligence tests are the Binet-Simon scale, the Stanford-Binet Intelligence Scale, and the Wechsler Adult Intelligence Scale.

The Binet-Simon Scale

Alfred Binet and his colleague **Theodore Simon** devised this general test of mental ability in 1905, and it was revised in 1908 and 1911. The test yielded scores in terms of mental age. Mental age is the chronological age that typically corresponds to a particular level of performance.

The Stanford-Binet Intelligence Scale

In 1916, **Lewis Terman** and his colleagues at Stanford University created the Stanford-Binet Intelligence Scale by expanding and revising the Binet-Simon scale. The Stanford-Binet yielded scores in terms of intelligence quotients. The **intelligence quotient (IQ)** is the mental age divided by the chronological age and multiplied by 100. IQ scores allowed children of different ages to be compared.

Wechsler Adult Intelligence Scale

David Wechsler published the first test for assessing intelligence in adults in 1939. The Wechsler Adult Intelligence Scale contains many items that assess nonverbal reasoning ability and therefore depends less on verbal ability that does the Stanford-Binet. It also provides separate scores of verbal intelligence and nonverbal or performance intelligence, as well as a score that indicates overall intelligence.

The term *intelligence quotient*, or IQ, is also used to describe the score on the Wechsler test. However, the Wechsler test presented scores based on a normal distribution of data rather than the intelligence quotient. The **normal distribution** is a symmetrical bell-shaped curve that represents how characteristics like IQ are distributed in a large population. In this scoring system, the mean IQ score is set at 100, and the standard deviation is set at 15. The test is constructed so that about two-thirds of people tested (68 percent) will score within one standard deviation of the mean, or between 85 and 115.

On the Wechsler test, the IQ score reflects where a person falls in the normal distribution of IQ scores. Therefore, this score, like the original Stanford-Binet IQ score, is a relative score, indicating how the test taker's score compares to the scores of other people. Most current intelligence tests, including the revised versions of the Stanford-Binet, now have scoring systems based on the normal distribution. About 95 percent of the population will score between 70 and 130 (within two standard deviations from the mean), and about 99.7 percent of the population will score between 55 and 145 (within three standard deviations from the mean).

Group Intelligence Tests

Individual intelligence tests can be given only by specially trained psychologists. Such tests are expensive and time-consuming to administer, and so educational institutions often use tests that can be given to a group of people at the same time. Commonly used group intelligence tests include the Otis-Lennon School Ability Test and the Lorge-Thorndike Intelligence Test.

Biological Tests of Intelligence

Some researchers have suggested that biological indices such as reaction time and perceptual speed relate to intelligence as measured by IQ tests:

- **Reaction time:** the amount of time a subject takes to respond to a stimulus, such as by pushing a button when a light is presented.

- **Perceptual speed:** the amount of time a person takes to accurately perceive and discriminate between stimuli. For example, a test of perceptual speed might require a person to determine which of two lines is shorter when pairs of lines flash very briefly on a screen.

The Influence of Culture

Many psychologists believe that cultural bias can affect intelligence tests, for the following reasons:

- Tests that are constructed primarily by white, middle-class researchers may not be equally relevant to people of all ethnic groups and economic classes.
- Cultural values and experiences can affect factors such as attitude toward exams, degree of comfort in the test setting, motivation, competitiveness, rapport with the test administrator, and comfort with problem solving independently rather than as part of a team effort.
- Cultural stereotypes can affect the motivation to perform well on tests.

Influence of Heredity and Environment

Today, researchers generally agree that heredity and environment have an interactive influence on intelligence. Many researchers believe that there is a **reaction range** to IQ, which refers to the limits placed on IQ by heredity. Heredity places an upper and lower limit on the IQ that can be attained by a given person. The environment determines where within these limits the person's IQ will lie.

Despite the prevailing view that both heredity and environment influence intelligence, researchers still have different opinions about how much each contributes and how they interact.

Hereditary Influences

Evidence for hereditary influences on intelligence comes from the following observations:

- Family studies show that intelligence tends to run in families.
- Twin studies show a higher correlation between identical twins in IQ than between fraternal twins. This holds true even when identical twins reared apart are compared to fraternal twins reared together.
- Adoption studies show that adopted children somewhat resemble their biological parents in intelligence.

Heritability of Intelligence

Heritability is a mathematical estimate that indicates how much of a trait's variation in a population can be attributed to genes. Estimates of the heritability of intelligence vary, depending on the methods used. Most researchers believe that heritability of intelligence is between 60 percent and 80 percent.

Heritability estimates apply only to groups on which the estimates are based. So far, heritability estimates have been based mostly on studies using white, middle-class subjects. Even if heritability of IQ is high, heredity does not necessarily account for differences *between* groups.

Environmental Influences

Evidence for environmental influences on intelligence comes from the following observations:

- Adoption studies demonstrate that adopted children show some similarity in IQ to their adoptive parents.
- Adoption studies also show that siblings reared together are more similar in IQ than siblings reared apart. This is true even when identical twins reared together are compared to identical twins reared apart.
- Biologically unrelated children raised together in the same home have some similarity in IQ.
- IQ declines over time in children raised in deprived environments, such as understaffed orphanages or circumstances of poverty and isolation. Conversely, IQ improves in children who leave deprived environments and enter enriched environments.

- People's performance on IQ tests has improved over time in industrialized countries. This strange phenomenon, which is known as the **Flynn effect**, is attributed to environmental influences.

Cultural and Ethnic Differences

Studies have shown a discrepancy in average IQ scores between whites and minority groups in the United States. Black, Native American, and Hispanic people score lower, on average, than white people on standardized IQ tests. Controversy exists about whether this difference is due to heredity or environment.

Hereditary Explanations

A few well-known proponents support hereditary explanations for cultural and ethnic differences in IQ:

- In the late 1960s, researcher Arthur Jensen created a storm of controversy by proposing that ethnic differences in intelligence are due to heredity. He based his argument on his own estimate of about 80 percent heritability for intelligence.
- In the 1990s, researchers Richard Herrnstein and Charles Murray created a similar controversy with their book, *The Bell Curve*. They also suggested that intelligence is largely inherited and that heredity at least partly contributes to ethnic and cultural differences.

Environmental Explanations

Many researchers believe that environmental factors primarily cause cultural and ethnic differences. They argue that because of a history of discrimination, minority groups comprise a disproportionately large part of the lower social classes, and therefore cultural and ethnic differences in intelligence are really differences among social classes. People in lower social classes have a relatively deprived environment. Children may have:

- Fewer learning resources
- Less privacy for study

- Less parental assistance
- Poorer role models
- Lower-quality schools
- Less motivation to excel intellectually

Some researchers argue that IQ tests are biased against some minority groups and thus cause the apparent cultural and ethnic differences.

Summary

Theories of Intelligence
- Intelligence is the capacity to acquire and apply knowledge.
- Intelligence includes the ability to benefit from experience, act purposefully, solve problems, and adapt to new situations.
- Charles Spearman proposed a general intelligence factor that underlies all intelligent behavior.
- Howard Gardner proposed that there are eight domains of intelligence.
- Robert Sternberg distinguished among three aspects of intelligence.
- Emotional intelligence helps people to perceive, express, understand, and regulate emotions.

Intelligence Testing
- The most commonly used individual tests of intelligence are the Binet-Simon scale, the Stanford-Binet Scale, and the Wechsler Adult Intelligence Scale.
- The Binet-Simon scale yielded scores in terms of mental age.
- The original Stanford-Binet test yielded scores in terms of intelligence quotient, or IQ.
- The Wechsler test yields scores based on a normal distribution.
- Although the term IQ is still used, current intelligence tests present

scores based on a normal distribution.
- Group intelligence tests are often used in educational settings.
- Some researchers have suggested that there are biological indices of intelligence, such as reaction time and perceptual speed.
- Many psychologists believe that cultural bias affects intelligence tests.

The Influence of Heredity and Environment

- There is dispute about how and how much heredity and environment affect intelligence.
- Evidence for hereditary influences come from family studies, twin studies, and adoption studies.
- Heritability estimates for intelligence vary depending on the method used for estimation.
- Evidence for environmental influences comes from adoption studies, studies of environmental deprivation, and the Flynn effect.
- There is probably a reaction range for IQ. Reaction range refers to limits set on IQ by heredity. Environment determines where IQ will lie within these limits.
- There is a discrepancy in IQ scores between whites and some minority groups.
- There are both hereditary and environmental explanations for this discrepancy.

CHAPTER 7:
Emotion

The source of our emotions remains elusive. No one knows exactly where emotions come from, what makes us feel the way we do, or whether we can fully control the way we feel. Emotion is intimately related to cognition and culture, and it affects us physically: our bodies react to different emotional states, and we often show emotion physically. Researchers have proposed many theories about the source, purpose, and expression of emotion.

In many ways, our emotions define our existence—without them, most of us would not feel truly alive. We've all felt fear of a lurking stranger, pride at scoring well on a test, love, sadness, and loneliness. And between emotional extremes are the ups and downs of everyday life: frustration in a traffic jam, contentment over a satisfying lunch, amusement at a cartoon. We have much to learn about emotion—but we have also learned simply by being human and feeling things every day.

Theories of Emotion

Emotion is a complex, subjective experience that is accompanied by biological and behavioral changes. Emotion involves feeling, thinking, activation of the nervous system, physiological changes, and behavioral changes such as facial expressions. Different theories exist regarding how and why people experience emotion. These include evolutionary theories, the **James-Lange theory**, the **Cannon-Bard theory**, Schacter and Singer's **two-factor theory**, and **cognitive appraisal**.

Evolutionary Theories

In the 1870s, **Charles Darwin** proposed that emotions evolved because they had adaptive value. For example, fear evolved because it helped people to act in ways that enhanced their chances of survival. Darwin believed that facial expressions of emotion are innate (hard-wired). He pointed out that facial expressions allow people to quickly judge someone's hostility or friendliness and to communicate intentions to others.

Recent evolutionary theories also consider emotions to be innate responses to stimuli. Evolutionary theorists tend to downplay the influence of thought and learning on emotion, although they acknowledge that both can have an effect. Evolutionary theorists believe that all human cultures share several primary emotions, including happiness, contempt, surprise, disgust, anger, fear, and sadness. They believe that all other emotions result from blends and different intensities of these primary emotions.

The James-Lange Theory

In the 1880s, two theorists, psychologist **William James** and physiologist **Carl Lange**, independently proposed an idea that challenged commonsense beliefs about emotion. This idea, which came to be known as the **James-Lange theory**, is that people experience emotion because they perceive their bodies' physiological responses to external events. According to this theory, people don't cry because they feel sad. Rather, people feel sad because they cry, and, likewise, they feel happy because they smile.

The Cannon-Bard Theory

The physiologist Walter Cannon disagreed with the James-Lange theory, posing three main arguments against it:

1. People can experience physiological arousal without experiencing emotion, such as when they have been running.
2. Physiological reactions happen too slowly to cause experiences of emotion, which occur very rapidly. For example, when someone is in a dark alley alone, a sudden sound usually provokes an immediate experience of fear, while the physical "symptoms" of fear generally follow that feeling.

3. People can experience very different emotions even when they have the same pattern of physiological arousal. For example, a person may have a racing heart and rapid breathing both when he is angry and when he is afraid.

Cannon proposed his own theory of emotion in the 1920s, which was extended by another physiologist, **Philip Bard,** in the 1930s. The resulting **Cannon-Bard theory** states that the experience of emotion happens at the same time that physiological arousal happens. Neither one causes the other. The brain gets a message that causes the experience of emotion at the same time that the autonomic nervous system gets a message that causes physiological arousal.

Schachter and Singer's Two-Factor Theory

In the 1960s, **Stanley Schachter** and **Jerome Singer** proposed a different theory to explain emotion. They said that people's experience of emotion depends on two factors: physiological arousal and the cognitive interpretation of that arousal. When people perceive physiological symptoms of arousal, they look for an environmental explanation of this arousal. The label people give an emotion depends on what they find in their environment.

Cognitive Appraisal

The psychologist **Richard Lazarus**'s research has shown that people's experience of emotion depends on the way they appraise or evaluate the events around them.

The Biological Bases of Emotion

The experience of emotion is accompanied by activation of two major areas of the nervous system: the brain and the autonomic nervous system.

Activation of Brain Regions

The area of the brain known as the **limbic system** is highly involved in emotion. One structure in the limbic system, called the **amygdala**, plays a particularly important role in regulating emotion.

Researchers believe that sensory information about emotion-evoking events moves along two pathways in the brain. The information goes first to the thalamus and from there moves simultaneously to the amygdala and the cortex of the brain. The amygdala processes the information quickly and sends signals to the hypothalamus, which in turn activates the autonomic nervous system. The cortex, on the other hand, processes the information more slowly, allowing people to appraise or evaluate the event.

Measuring Emotion

Researchers often use autonomic responses to measure emotion. One frequently used autonomic response is called the galvanic skin response. The **galvanic skin response** is an increase in the skin's rate of electrical conductivity, which occurs when subjects sweat during emotional states. Researchers also use indicators such as blood pressure, muscle tension, heart rate, and respiration rate to measure emotion.

Expression of Emotion

People express emotions not only through speech but also through nonverbal behavior, or body language. Nonverbal behavior includes facial expressions, postures, and gestures.

The Basic Emotions

The psychologist **Paul Ekman** and his colleagues have identified six basic emotions: happiness, sadness, anger, fear, surprise, and disgust. Worldwide, most people can identify the facial expressions that correspond to these emotions.

The Facial-Feedback Hypothesis

Some researchers have proposed that the brain uses feedback from facial muscles to recognize emotions that are being experienced. This idea is known as the **facial-feedback hypothesis**. It follows from this hypothesis that making the facial expression corresponding to a particular emotion can make a person feel that emotion.

Studies have shown that this phenomenon does indeed occur. For example, if people smile and try to look happy, they will feel happiness to some degree.

Gender Differences

Some research suggests that the genders differ in how much emotion they express. In North America, women appear to display more emotion than men. Anger is an exception—men tend to express anger more than women, particularly toward strangers. This gender difference in expressiveness is not absolute. It depends on gender roles, cultural norms, and context.

Emotion and Culture

Some aspects of emotion are universal to all cultures, while other aspects differ across cultures.

Similarities Among Cultures

Ekman and his colleagues have found that people in different cultures can identify the six basic emotions: happiness, sadness, anger, fear, surprise, and disgust. The physiological indicators of emotion are similar in people from different cultures.

Differences Among Cultures

Although many emotions and expressions of emotions are universal, some differences exist among cultures:

- **Categories of emotions:** People in different cultures categorize emotions differently. Some languages have labels for emotions that are not labeled in other languages.
- **Prioritization of emotions:** Different cultures consider different emotions to be primary.
- **Different emotions evoked:** The same situation may evoke different emotions in different cultures.
- **Differences in nonverbal expressions:** Nonverbal expressions of emotion differ across cultures, due partly to the fact that different cultures have different display rules. **Display rules** are norms that tell people whether, which, how, and when emotions should be displayed.
- **Power of cultural norms:** Cultural norms determine how and when to show emotions that are not actually felt. Acting out an emotion that is not felt is called **emotion work**.

Happiness

Happiness is a basic human emotion, but people often make assumptions about happiness that empirical research does not support. For example, people often assume that most people feel unhappy and dissatisfied with their lives, but research shows this is not true. Most people describe themselves as fairly happy even if they are in less-than-ideal circumstances. Surprisingly, researchers have not found a consistent positive correlation between happiness and factors such as wealth, age, intelligence, physical attractiveness, or parenthood—factors that many people commonly associate with happiness.

Although circumstances do not reliably predict happiness, some circumstances do correlate with increased happiness. These include having a good social network, being married, having a satisfying job, and having strong religious convictions. These circumstances, however, are only correlated with happiness. Research also shows that happiness tends to depend on people's expectations of life and on how people compare themselves to their peers.

Rather than focusing only on negative reactions to unfavorable circumstances, researchers today have begun to study **subjective well-being**. Subjective well-being is the perception people have about their happiness and satisfaction with life. Subjective well-being depends more on attitudes to external circumstances than on the circumstances themselves. That is, factors such as wealth or employment don't matter as much as how we feel about our wealth or employment.

Summary

Theories of Emotion

- Emotion is a complex, subjective experience that is accompanied by biological and behavioral changes.
- Charles Darwin proposed that emotional expressions are hard-wired and that emotions evolved because they had adaptive value.
- Current evolutionary theorists believe that emotions are innate.
- The James-Lange theory states that people experience emotion because they perceive their bodies' physiological responses to external events.
- The Cannon-Bard theory states that the experience of emotion and the accompanying physiological arousal happen at the same time.
- Schachter and Singer's two-factor theory states that people's experience of emotion depends on physiological arousal and the cognitive interpretation of that arousal.
- People's experience of emotion depends on how they evaluate their environment.

The Biological Bases of Emotion

- Emotion involves activation of the brain and the autonomic nervous system.

- Information about emotion-evoking events moves along two pathways in the brain.
- The pathway to the amygdala allows people to respond rapidly to events.
- The pathway to the cortex allows people to appraise events more slowly.
- Researchers use autonomic responses to measure emotion.

Expression of Emotion

- People worldwide can identify six primary emotions: happiness, sadness, anger, fear, surprise, and disgust.
- The facial-feedback hypothesis states that the brain uses feedback from facial muscles to recognize emotions that are being experienced.
- The two genders express different amounts of emotion. This difference depends on gender roles, culture, and context.

Emotion and Culture

- People in different cultures can identify six basic emotions.
- There are universal physiological indicators of emotion.
- People in different cultures categorize emotions differently.
- The same situation may evoke different emotions in different cultures.
- Nonverbal expressions of emotion differ across cultures.
- Cultural norms determine how and when to display emotions that are not actually felt.

Happiness

- Subjective well-being depends more on attitudes toward circumstances than on the circumstances themselves.
- Happiness tends to depend on people's expectations of life and on the way they compare themselves to others.

CHAPTER 8:
Motivation

Motivation is an internal process that makes a person move toward a goal. Motivation, like intelligence, can't be directly observed. Instead, motivation can only be inferred by noting a person's behavior.

Researchers have proposed theories that try to explain human motivation. These theories include **drive reduction theories** and Maslow's **hierarchy of needs theory**.

Drive Reduction Theories

Drive reduction theories of motivation suggest that people act in order to reduce needs and maintain a constant physiological state. For example, people eat in order to reduce their need for food. The idea of homeostasis is central to drive reduction theories. **Homeostasis** is the maintenance of a state of physiological equilibrium.

Drive reduction theories fail to explain several aspects of motivation:

- People sometimes aren't motivated by internal needs.
- Sometimes, people continue being motivated even when they have satisfied internal needs.
- People are often motivated by external incentives as well as internal needs.

Intrinsic and Extrinsic Motivation

A motivation may be intrinsic, extrinsic, or both. **Intrinsic motivation** is the motivation to act for the sake of the activity alone. For example, people have intrinsic motivation to write poetry if they do it simply because they enjoy it. **Extrinsic motivation**, on the other hand, is the motivation to act for external rewards. For example, people have extrinsic motivation to write if they do so in the hopes of getting published, being famous, or making money.

Maslow's Hierarchy Of Needs

In the 1970s, the psychologist **Abraham Maslow** suggested that people are motivated by a **hierarchy of needs**:

- First, most basic level: physiological needs, such as the need for food, water, safety, and security
- Second level: needs for social interaction, such as the need to belong
- Third level: needs for esteem, which include the need for respect from oneself and others
- Fourth level: needs for self-actualization, or realizing one's full potential

Maslow believed people pay attention to higher needs only when lower needs are satisfied. Critics argue that Maslow's theory doesn't explain why higher needs often motivate people even when lower needs are unsatisfied.

Types of Needs

People have innate needs and learned needs, both of which are influenced by society and culture. People have a limited number of innate needs, which include needs for food, water, oxygen, and elimination of wastes. There are, however, a relatively large number of learned needs, including needs for achievement, autonomy, and power. These needs are determined by **values**, or people's perceptions of what is important in life.

Hunger

Hunger is a complicated motivation; people don't eat only because they need food. Many factors, both biological and environmental, influence hunger. These factors interact with one another in many ways.

Biological Factors

Researchers believe certain genetic differences among individuals play a role in hunger. The brain, the digestive system, and hormones are all involved in influencing hunger at the biological level.

Environmental Factors

Many environmental factors influence hunger, including the availability of rich foods, taste preferences, habits, memory, stress, and cultural attitudes.

Sexual Drive

Unlike hunger, sexual drive does not motivate people to fulfill a basic biological need. A lack of food leads to death; a lack of sex, on the other hand, does not. Both biological and psychological factors strongly influence sexual drive.

Kinsey's Studies

One of the first researchers to give a modern account of human sexuality was **Alfred Kinsey**. In the 1940s, he and his colleagues interviewed more than 18,000 U.S. men and women about their sexual behavior and attitudes. In his comprehensive reports about human sexuality, Kinsey denounced the repressive social attitudes of his time, which he said bore little relation to actual sexual practices. Kinsey provided statistics showing that sexual practices varied widely and that even in the 1940s there was a high prevalence of masturbation and premarital sex.

Masters and Johnson's Studies

Other pioneers of sexual research were **William Masters** and **Virginia Johnson**. In the 1960s, they studied several hundred male and female volunteers who agreed to either masturbate or have intercourse in a laboratory. Masters and Johnson hooked up the volunteers to instruments that measured various physiological indicators during sexual activity. Using the results of these studies, they described the sexual response cycle.

The Sexual Response Cycle

Masters and Johnson divided the human sexual response cycle into four phases:

1. **Excitement phase:** Physiological arousal increases quickly. Muscle tension, heart rate, blood pressure, and breathing rate increase. In

men, the penis gets erect and the testes swell. In women, the clitoris hardens and swells, the vaginal lips open, and the vagina lubricates.

2. **Plateau phase:** Physiological arousal continues. In women, the clitoris retracts under the clitoral hood. Men may secrete a small amount of fluid from the penis.

3. **Orgasm phase:** Physiological arousal peaks. Men ejaculate seminal fluid. Both men and women experience muscular contractions in the pelvic area, along with a sensation of pleasure.

4. **Resolution phase:** Physiological responses return to normal levels. Men then go through a refractory period that can vary in length, during which they are not responsive to stimulation. The refractory period tends to get longer as men age.

Psychological Factors in Sexual Motivation

Hormones alone cannot cause sexual arousal. Psychological factors are also highly influential.

- **Erotic stimuli:** Both men and women can become sexually aroused by external and internal erotic stimuli. External erotic stimuli include sexually exciting material that is read, heard, or seen. Internal erotic stimuli include thoughts, fantasies, and memories of past sexual experiences.

- **Desires:** People have an infinite number of desires that influence the motivation for sex, including to procreate, to express love, to have physical enjoyment, to cope with difficult situations and emotions, to validate one's desirability, and to do what peers do.

- **Cultural context:** Cultures inform people about sexual scripts, or implicit rules that allow a person to judge the appropriate sexual behavior for a given situation. For example, people follow sexual scripts when deciding whether they should initiate sexual activity or wait to receive a partner's advances.

Gender Differences in Sexual Behavior and Partner Choice

Many researchers have found that some differences exist between men and women in sexual behavior and partner choice, though all men and all women do not behave the same way or feel the same things.

Men	Women
More interested in sex; initiate and think about sex more often	Less interested in sex
Want sex with more partners	Not as interested in sex with many partners
Desire sex without emotional commitment	Desire sex with emotional commitment
Focus on youth and physical attractiveness when choosing a sex partner	Focus on social and economic status when choosing a sex partner
Feel more jealous when partner is physically unfaithful	Feel more jealous when partner is emotionally unfaithful

Evolutionary Explanations

Some theorists use evolutionary theory to explain these gender differences. Their explanations are generally based on Robert Trivers's idea that men and women make different parental investments in order to produce offspring. From a biological standpoint, men invest no more than the energy required for intercourse. Women, on the other hand, invest time and energy in pregnancy and breast-feeding.

Males can increase their reproductive success by producing as many offspring as possible. Evolutionary theory predicts that men tend to choose attractive, youthful partners because these qualities imply good health and an ability to reproduce successfully. Females increase their reproductive success by being highly discriminating when choosing mates. They try to select males who have the most access to material resources, because such males can contribute the most to caring for offspring.

Furthermore, men must contend with paternity uncertainty—they can never be certain that they are the fathers of their partners' offspring. Evolutionary theorists predict that men would therefore tend to have concerns about their partners' sexual infidelity. Women, on the other hand, *can* be certain that their offspring are their own, though they cannot be certain that their partners will provide for their offspring. Therefore, they are more likely to be concerned about the emotional fidelity of their partners.

Sexual Orientation

Sexual orientation is such a controversial subject that people cannot even agree about how the term *sexual orientation* should be defined. Some people argue over whether it refers to sexual behavior, sexual attraction, emotional attraction, or all three.

Researchers define sexual orientation in a variety of ways, which means there is no clear idea about what proportion of the population is homosexual. Researchers also have many different opinions regarding how much biological and environmental factors contribute to sexual orientation.

Possible Biological Factors

Researchers have many ideas about the possible biological factors of homosexuality:

- **Hormones:** Some researchers have suggested that homosexuals and heterosexuals have different levels of various hormones in the blood. However, research in this area has failed consistently to find hormonal variations that could account for differences in sexual orientation.
- **Genes:** Others have proposed that there is a genetic basis for predisposition to homosexuality. To investigate the possibility of a genetic basis, researchers have studied the sexual orientations of the

identical, fraternal, and adoptive siblings of homosexual people. This research has shown that the identical twins of homosexuals are much more likely to be homosexual than the fraternal twins of homosexuals. In turn, the fraternal twins of homosexuals are more likely to be homosexual than the adoptive siblings of homosexuals.

- **Prenatal factors:** Some researchers have focused on prenatal environment. These researchers believe that the level of hormones present during a critical period in prenatal development can affect the organization of the brain, which in turn can influence sexual orientation. Research shows that women who were exposed to high prenatal levels of androgens are more likely to be homosexual.
- **Brain differences:** One researcher, Simon LeVay, examined anatomical differences in the brains of homosexual and heterosexual men. He found that a specific area of the hypothalamus tended to be smaller in homosexual men and in heterosexual women than in heterosexual men.

Environmental Factors

Many researchers believe biological factors alone can't explain the origin of homosexuality. For example, there is only about a 50 percent chance that the identical twins of homosexual men will also be homosexual. Therefore, some other factor must make the other 50 percent heterosexual. Although this other factor remains unknown, researchers have proposed a number of environmental situations that might influence sexual orientation:

- An ineffectual, distant father and an overly close, domineering mother
- Seduction in childhood by a homosexual adult
- Same-sex sexual play as children

However, many of these proposals lack empirical support.

Achievement

An **achievement motive** is an impulse to master challenges and reach a high standard of excellence. Both personality and situational factors influence achievement motivation.

Researchers often use the **Thematic Apperception Test (TAT)** to measure people's need for achievement. The TAT consists of a set of ambiguous pictures, such as one of a woman standing in the doorway of a room. Researchers ask subjects to make up stories about these pictures. Some subjects' stories consistently contain themes that relate to achievement. Researchers consider these subjects to have a high need for achievement.

Personality Factors

High-achievement motivation tends to lead to particular personality features. These include persistence, ability to delay gratification, and competitiveness.

Situational Factors

Some situational factors also affect achievement motivation. They include the expectation of success, incentives, control, and opportunity.

Summary

What Is Motivation?

- Motivation is an internal process that makes a person move toward a goal.
- Motivation may be extrinsic, intrinsic, or both.
- Drive reduction theories of motivation suggest that people act in order to reduce needs and maintain a constant physiological state.

- Abraham Maslow proposed that there is a hierarchy of needs and that people pay attention to higher needs only when lower ones are satisfied.
- Needs may be innate or learned. Learned needs are determined by values. Both innate and learned needs are influenced by society and culture.

Hunger

- The brain, the digestive system and hormones regulate hunger.
- Environmental influences on hunger include availability of foods, preferences, habits, memory, stress, and cultural attitudes.

Sexual Drive

- Alfred Kinsey was one of the first people to give a modern account of human sexuality.
- William Masters and Virginia Johnson described the human sexual response.
- The sexual response cycle has four phases: excitement, plateau, orgasm, and resolution.
- Psychological influences on sex drive include internal and external erotic stimuli, desires, and cultural context.
- Researchers have found that there are some gender differences in sexual behavior and partner choice. Both evolutionary and sociocultural explanations can account for these differences.
- Estimates of the prevalence of homosexuality vary, and the causes of homosexuality remain unclear.
- Researchers have suggested that biological factors including hormone levels, genes, prenatal environment, and brain anatomy could influence sexual orientation.
- Psychologists have proposed several theories about how environment might influence homosexuality, but research has failed to support these theories.

Achievement

- Researchers often use the thematic apperception test (TAT) to measure the need for achievement.
- People who have a high achievement motivation tend to be persistent and hardworking. They are able to delay gratification to meet long-term goals, and they tend to choose careers that allow them to compete with others.

CHAPTER 9:
Personality

What does it mean to have "personality"? Someone with personality could be funny, passionate, daring, extroverted, aggressive, egotistical, hot-tempered, or insecure. He or she might be altruistic, humble, mellow, shy, or wary. He or she might even be all or any of these things at different times and in different places, depending on the situation. Researchers have developed many ways of assessing personality, but even if we do gain an understanding of how we are, the question of why we're that way remains.

Personality Traits

Personality is the collection of characteristic thoughts, feelings, and behaviors that are associated with a person. Personality **traits** are characteristic behaviors and feelings that are consistent and long lasting.

Ancient Greek Ideas

The ancient Greeks believed that people's personalities depended on the kind of **humor**, or fluid, most prevalent in their bodies. The ancient Greeks identified four humors—blood, phlegm, black bile, and yellow bile—and categorized people's personalities to correspond as follows:

- **Sanguine:** blood; cheerful and passionate
- **Phlegmatic:** phlegm; dull and unemotional
- **Melancholic:** black bile; unhappy and depressed
- **Choleric:** yellow bile; angry and hot-tempered

The Greek theory of personality remained influential well into the eighteenth century.

Cattell's Sixteen Traits

Like the ancient Greeks, modern researchers believe in the existence of a few basic personality traits. Combinations of these basic traits, they believe, form other traits. Psychologist Raymond Cattell used a statistical procedure called **factor analysis** to identify basic personality traits from a very long list of English words that identified traits. Factor analysis allowed Cattell to cluster these traits into groups according to their similarities. He found that personality is made up of sixteen basic dimensions.

The Big Five Traits

Other researchers have since clustered personality traits into even fewer categories. Today, many psychologists believe that all personality traits derive from five basic personality traits, which are commonly referred to as the **Big Five**:

1. Neuroticism
2. Extraversion
3. Openness to experience
4. Agreeableness
5. Conscientiousness

The Big Five traits remain quite stable over the life span, particularly after the age of thirty. Although researchers identified the Big Five traits by using a list of English words, these traits seem to be applicable in many countries.

Psychodynamic Theories

Many psychologists have proposed theories that try to explain the origins of personality. One highly influential set of theories stems from the work of Austrian neurologist **Sigmund Freud**, who first proposed the theory of psychoanalysis. Collectively, these theories are known as **psychodynamic theories**. Although many different psychodynamic theories exist, they all emphasize unconscious motives and desires, as well as the importance of childhood experiences in shaping personality.

Sigmund Freud's Theory of Psychoanalysis

In the late 1800s and early 1900s, Freud developed a technique that he called **psychoanalysis** and used it to treat mental disorders. He formed his theory of psychoanalysis by observing his patients. According to psychoanalytic theory, personalities arise because of attempts to resolve conflicts between unconscious sexual and aggressive impulses and societal demands to restrain these impulses.

The Conscious, the Preconscious, and the Unconscious

Freud believed that most mental processes are unconscious. He proposed that people have three levels of awareness:

- The **conscious** contains all the information that a person is paying attention to at any given time.
- The **preconscious** contains all the information outside of a person's attention but readily available if needed.
- The **unconscious** contains thoughts, feelings, desires, and memories of which people have no awareness but that influence every aspect of their day-to-day lives.

Freud believed that information in the unconscious emerges in slips of the tongue, jokes, dreams, illness symptoms, and the associations people make between ideas.

The Id, the Ego, and the Superego

Freud proposed that personalities have three components: the id, the ego, and the superego.

- **Id:** a reservoir of instinctual energy that contains biological urges such as impulses toward survival, sex, and aggression. The id is unconscious and operates according to the **pleasure principle**, the drive to achieve pleasure and avoid pain. The id is characterized by **primary process thinking**, which is illogical, irrational, and motivated by a desire for the immediate gratification of impulses.

- **Ego:** the component that manages the conflict between the id and the constraints of the real world. Some parts of the ego are unconscious, while others are preconscious or conscious. The ego operates according to the **reality principle,** the awareness that gratification of impulses has to be delayed in order to accommodate the demands of the real world. The ego is characterized by **secondary process thinking,** which is logical and rational. The ego's role is to prevent the id from gratifying its impulses in socially inappropriate ways.

- **Superego:** the moral component of personality. It contains all the moral standards learned from parents and society. The superego forces the ego to conform not only to reality but also to its ideals of morality. Hence, the superego causes people to feel guilty when they go against society's rules. Like the ego, the superego operates at all three levels of awareness.

Conflict

Freud believed that the id, the ego, and the superego are in constant conflict. He focused mainly on conflicts concerning sexual and aggressive urges because these urges are most likely to violate societal rules.

Anxiety

Internal conflicts can make a person feel anxious. In Freud's view, anxiety arises when the ego cannot adequately balance the demands of the id and the superego. The id demands gratification of its impulses, and the superego demands maintenance of its moral standards.

Defense Mechanisms

To manage these internal conflicts, people use defense mechanisms. **Defense mechanisms** are behaviors that protect people from anxiety. There are many different kinds of defense mechanisms, many of which are automatic and unconscious:

- **Repression:** keeping unpleasant thoughts, memories, and feelings shut up in the unconscious
- **Reaction formation:** behaving in a way that is opposite to behavior, feelings, or thoughts that are considered unacceptable
- **Projection:** attributing one's own unacceptable thoughts or feelings to someone else
- **Rationalization:** using incorrect but self-serving explanations to justify unacceptable behavior, thoughts, or feelings
- **Displacement:** transferring feelings about a person or event onto someone or something else
- **Denial:** refusing to acknowledge something that is obvious to others
- **Regression:** reverting to a more immature state of psychological development
- **Sublimation:** channeling unacceptable thoughts and feelings into socially acceptable behavior

Psychosexual Stages of Development

Freud believed that personality solidifies during childhood, largely before age five. He proposed five stages of psychosexual development: the oral stage, the anal stage, the phallic stage, the latency stage, and the genital stage. He believed that at each stage of development, children gain sexual gratification, or sensual pleasure, from a particular part of their bodies. Each stage has special conflicts, and children's ways of managing these conflicts influence their personalities.

If a child's needs in a particular stage are gratified too much or frustrated too much, the child can become fixated at that stage of development. **Fixation** is an inability to progress normally from one stage into another. When the child becomes an adult, the fixation shows up as a tendency to focus on the needs that were overgratified or overfrustrated.

Freud's Psychosexual Stages of Development			
Stage	**Age**	**Sources of pleasure**	**Result of fixation**
Oral stage	Birth to roughly twelve months	Activities involving the mouth, such as sucking, biting, and chewing	Excessive smoking, overeating, or dependence on others.
Anal stage	Age two, when the child is being toilet trained	Bowel movements	An overly controlling (anal-retentive) personality or an easily angered (anal-expulsive personality)
Phallic Stage	Age three to five	The genitals	Guilt or anxiety about sex
Latency Stage	Age five to puberty	Sexuality is latent, or dormant, during this period	No fixations at this stage
Genital stage	Begins at puberty	The genitals; sexual urges return	No fixations at this stage

Carl Jung's Analytical Psychology

Until the 1910s, **Carl Jung** was a follower and close friend of Freud's. Like Freud, Jung believed that unconscious conflicts are important in shaping personality. However, he believed the unconscious has two layers: the **personal unconscious**, which resembled Freud's idea, and the collective **unconscious**, which contains universal memories of the common human past.

Jung called these common memories archetypes. **Archetypes** are images or thoughts that have the same meaning for all human beings. Jung said that archetypes exist in dreams as well as in art, literature, and religion across cultures.

Alfred Adler's Individual Psychology

Alfred Adler, another follower of Freud and a member of his inner circle, eventually broke away from Freud and developed his own school of thought, which he called **individual psychology**. Adler believed that the main motivations for human behavior are not sexual or aggressive urges but strivings for superiority. He pointed out that children naturally feel weak and inadequate in comparison to adults. This normal feeling of inferiority drives them to adapt, develop skills, and master challenges. Adler used the term *compensation* to refer to the attempt to shed normal feelings of inferiority.

However, some people suffer from an exaggerated sense of inferiority, or an **inferiority complex**, which can be due either to being spoiled or neglected by parents. Such people **overcompensate**, which means that rather than try to master challenges, they try to cover up their sense of inferiority by focusing on outward signs of superiority such as status, wealth, and power.

Object-Relations Theories

The object-relations school of psychoanalysis emerged in the 1950s, led by a group of psychoanalysts that included D. W. Winnicott and Melanie Klein. The term *object relations* refers to the relationships that people have with others, who are represented mentally as objects with certain attributes. Object-relations theorists believe that people are motivated most by attachments to others rather than by sexual and aggressive impulses. According to these theorists, the conflict between autonomy and the need for other people plays a key role in shaping personality.

Behaviorist Theories

The school of behaviorism emerged in the 1910s, led by **John B. Watson**. Unlike psychodynamic theorists, behaviorists study only observable behavior. Their explanations of personality focus on learning. Skinner, Albert Bandura, and Walter Mischel all proposed important behaviorist theories.

B. F. Skinner's Ideas

Skinner believed that the environment determines behavior. According to his view, people have consistent behavior patterns because they have particular kinds of **response tendencies**. This means that over time, people learn to behave in particular ways. Behaviors that have positive consequences tend to increase, while behaviors that have negative consequences tend to decrease.

Albert Bandura's Ideas

Albert Bandura pointed out that people learn to respond in particular ways by watching other people, who are called models. Although Bandura agrees that personality arises through learning, he believes that conditioning is not an automatic, mechanical process. He and other theorists believe that cognitive processes like thinking and reasoning are important in learning. The kind of behaviorism they advocate is called social-cognitive learning.

Walter Mischel's Ideas

Walter Mischel, like Bandura, is a social-cognitive theorist. Mischel's research showed that situations have a strong effect on people's behavior and that people's responses to situations depend on their thoughts about the likely consequences of their behavior. Mischel's research caused considerable debate because it cast doubt on the idea of stable personality traits. Mischel himself did not want to abandon the idea of stable personality traits. He believed that researchers should pay attention to both situational and personal characteristics that influence behavior.

Today, most psychologists acknowledge that both a person's characteristics and the specific situation at hand influence how a person behaves. Personal characteristics include innate temperaments, learned habits, and beliefs. The environment includes opportunities, rewards, punishments, and chance occurrences. Personality results from a two-way interaction between a person's characteristics and the environment. This process of interaction is called r**eciprocal determinism**. People's characteristics influence the kind of environment in which they find themselves. Those environments, in turn, influence and modify people's personal characteristics.

Humanistic Theories

Some psychologists at the time disliked psychodynamic and behaviorist explanations of personality. They felt that these theories ignored the qualities that make humans unique among animals, such as striving for self-determination and self-realization. In the 1950s, some of these psychologists began a school of psychology called **humanism**.

Humanistic psychologists try to see people's lives as those people would see them. They tend to have an optimistic perspective on human nature. They focus on the ability of human beings to think consciously and rationally, to control their biological urges, and to achieve their full potential. In the humanistic view, people are responsible for their lives and actions and have the freedom and will to change their attitudes and behavior.

Abraham Maslow's Theory

The highest rung on **Abraham Maslow**'s ladder of human motives is the need for self-actualization. Maslow said that human beings strive for **self-actualization**, or realization of their full potential, once they have satisfied their more basic needs.

Maslow also provided his own account of the healthy human personality. Psychodynamic theories tend to be based on clinical case studies and therefore lack accounts of healthy personalities. To come up with his account, Maslow studied exceptional historical figures, such as Abraham Lincoln and Eleanor Roosevelt, as well as some of his own contemporaries whom he thought had exceptionally good mental health.

Maslow described several characteristics that self-actualizing people share:

- Awareness and acceptance of themselves
- Openness and spontaneity

- The ability to enjoy work and see work as a mission to fulfill
- The ability to develop close friendships without being overly dependent on other people
- A good sense of humor
- The tendency to have peak experiences that are spiritually or emotionally satisfying

Carl Rogers's Person-Centered Theory

Carl Rogers, another humanistic psychologist, proposed a theory called the **person-centered theory**. Like Freud, Rogers drew on clinical case studies to come up with his theory. He also drew from the ideas of Maslow and others. In Rogers's view, the **self-concept** is the most important feature of personality, and it includes all the thoughts, feelings, and beliefs people have about themselves. Rogers believed that people are aware of their self-concepts.

Biological Approaches

Psychologists agree that environmental factors interact with genetic factors to form personality. Some psychologists have proposed theories that emphasize these genetic influences on personality.

Hans Eysenck's Theory

Psychologist **Hans Eysenck** believes that genetics are the primary determinate of personality, although he thinks conditioning also plays a role. According to Eysenck, personality traits are hierarchical, with a few basic traits giving rise to a large array of more superficial traits. Genetically determined differences in physiological functioning make some people more vulnerable to behavioral conditioning. Eysenck suggests that introverted people have higher levels of physiological arousal, which allows them to be conditioned by environmental stimuli more easily. Because of this, such people develop more inhibitions, which make them more shy and uneasy in social situations.

Environmental Influences

The environment also has important influences on personality. These include peer relationships and the kinds of situations a child encounters. As Walter Mischel believed, the interactions between innate characteristics and environmental factors are two-way. Children's temperaments are likely to influence their peer relationships and the situations they encounter. Similarly, peers and situations can modify children's personality characteristics.

Evolutionary Approaches

Evolutionary theorists explain personality in terms of its adaptive value. Theorists such as David Buss have argued that the Big Five personality traits are universally important because these traits have given humans a reproductive advantage.

Culture and Personality

Cultural psychologists have noted that some aspects of personality differ across cultural groups. For example, Americans and Asians have slightly different conceptions of self. American culture promotes a view of the self as independent. American children tend to describe themselves in terms of personal attributes, values, and achievements, and they learn to be self-reliant, to compete with others, and to value their uniqueness.

Many Asian cultures, such as those of Japan and China, promote a view of the self as interdependent. Children from these cultures tend to describe themselves in terms of which groups they belong to. They learn to rely on others, to be modest about achievements, and to fit into groups.

Researchers believe that culture influences aggressiveness in males. In places where there are plentiful resources and no serious threats to survival, such as Tahiti or Sudest Island near New Guinea, males are not socialized to be aggressive. Culture also influences altruism. Research shows that children tend to offer support or unselfish suggestions more frequently in cultures where they are expected to help with chores such as food preparation and caring for younger siblings.

Summary

Personality Traits

- Personality is the collection of characteristic thoughts, feelings, and behaviors that make up a person.
- Personality traits are consistent and long lasting, while states are temporary.
- The Greeks thought that four types of humors corresponded to personality types.
- Raymond Cattell used factor analysis to cluster traits into sixteen groups.
- Many psychologists believe that there are five basic traits.
- These Big Five traits include neuroticism, extraversion, openness to experience, agreeableness, and conscientiousness.

Psychodynamic Theories

- Psychodynamic theories are based on Sigmund Freud's theory of psychoanalysis and emphasize unconscious motives and the importance of childhood experiences in shaping personality.
- Freud believed that the mind has three levels of awareness: the conscious, the preconscious, and the unconscious.
- Information in the unconscious emerges in slips of the tongue, jokes, dreams, illness symptoms, and associations between ideas.
- The personality is made up of three components that are in constant conflict: the id (biological impulses), the ego (the reality principle), and the superego (moral component).
- Anxiety arises when the ego is unable to balance adequately the demands of the id and superego.
- People use defense mechanisms to protect themselves from anxiety.
- Freud proposed that children undergo five stages of development, each characterized by sexual gratification from a particular part of the body.
- Fixation is an inability to progress normally from one developmental stage to another.

- According to Carl Jung's analytical psychology, people have a personal unconscious and a collective unconscious. The latter contains universal memories of people's common human past.
- According to Alfred Adler's individual psychology, the main motivations for behavior are strivings for superiority.
- Object relations theorists believe that people are motivated most by attachments to people.

Behaviorist Theories

- Behaviorist explanations of personality focus on learning.
- B. F. Skinner believed that people's personalities arise from response tendencies and that consequences shape the responses.
- Albert Bandura said that people learn responses by watching others. He believes that thinking and reasoning are important in learning.
- Walter Mischel's research showed that people behave differently in different situations.
- Psychologists agree that personality is formed through a two-way interaction between personal characteristics and the environment. This interaction is called reciprocal determinism.

Humanistic Theories

- Humanistic theories emphasize subjective viewpoints when studying personality. They have an optimistic view that focuses on humans' rationality, consciousness, and freedom.
- Abraham Maslow studied the healthy personality and described the characteristics of the self-actualizing personality.
- Carl Rogers's person-centered theory suggests that the self-concept is the most important feature of personality. Children's self-concepts match reality if their parents give them unconditional love. Rogers said that people experience anxiety when reality threatens their self-concepts.

Biological Approaches

- Hans Eysenck believes that genetics largely determine personality.
- Studies of temperament and heritability provide the most empirical evidence for genetic contributions to personality.
- Environment influences peer relationships and situations.
- Sharing a family environment does not lead to many similarities in personality.
- Evolutionary theorists explain personality in terms of its adaptive value.

Culture and Personality

- American culture promotes a view of the self as independent, while Asian cultures generally promote a view of the self as interdependent.
- Culture influences both aggressiveness in males and altruism.
- Cultural psychologists face the challenge of avoiding stereotypes and acknowledging universal features while studying differences among cultures.

CHAPTER 10:
Stress, Coping, and Health

We all experience stress, but we don't all find the same situations stressful. Some people find flying in planes highly stressful, while others take up skydiving as a hobby. Some people thrive in fast-paced, deadline-heavy careers, while others prefer less stimulating work. Stress means different things for different people, and everyone has their own way of coping with it. In some cases, people can worry themselves sick— literally—and some research links stress directly to illness.

Today, most researchers use a biopsychosocial model to explain disease. According to the biopsychosocial model, physical illness results from a complicated interaction among biological, psychological, and sociocultural factors. In recent decades, the recognition that psychological factors can affect health has given rise to a new branch of psychology called health psychology. Health psychologists study the relationship between psychosocial factors and the emergence, progression, and treatment of illness.

Stress and Stressors

Stress is difficult to define because researchers approach it in different ways. Some use the term *stress* to refer to circumstances that threaten well-being or to refer to the response people have to threatening circumstances. Others think of stress as the process of evaluating and coping with threatening circumstances. Yet others use the term to refer to the experience of being threatened by taxing circumstances. This chapter will use the term *stress* in the last sense: the experience of being threatened by taxing circumstances.

Types of Stressors

Stressors are psychologically or physically demanding events or circumstances. Research links stressors to increased susceptibility to physical illnesses such as heart disease as well as to psychological problems such as anxiety and depression. Researchers who study stress usually distinguish among three types of stressors:

- **Catastrophic events:** large earthquakes, hurricanes, wars
- **Major life changes, positive or negative:** marriage, divorce, death of a parent, beginning a new job, starting college
- **Minor hassles:** standing in line, traffic jams, noisy environments

Internal Sources of Stress

Exposure to difficult circumstances doesn't produce stress by itself. Rather, stress occurs when people experience frustration, conflict, or pressure:

- **Frustration** is the experience of being thwarted when trying to achieve a goal.
- **Conflict** occurs when people have two or more incompatible desires or motives.
- **Pressure** occurs when people feel compelled to behave in a particular way because of expectations set by themselves or others.

The Physiology of Stress

The experience of stress is accompanied by many physiological changes.

Selye's General Adaptation Syndrome

Hans Selye, a pioneer in the field of stress research, proposed that stressors of many different kinds result in a nonspecific bodily response. He said the body's stress response consists of a **general adaptation syndrome**, which has three stages: alarm, resistance, and exhaustion.

STAGE 1

In the **alarm stage**, an organism recognizes a threatening situation. The sympathetic nervous system activates, giving rise to the fight-or-flight response. Digestive processes slow down, blood pressure and heart rate increase, adrenal hormones are released, and blood is drawn away from the skin to the skeletal muscles.

STAGE 2

The **resistance stage** occurs when stress continues. Physiological arousal stabilizes at a point that is higher than normal.

STAGE 3

If stress is prolonged, organisms reach the **exhaustion stage**. The body's resources run out, and physiological arousal decreases. In this stage, organisms become more susceptible to disease.

Coping

Coping refers to efforts to manage stress. Coping can be adaptive or maladaptive. Adaptive coping strategies generally involve confronting problems directly, making reasonably realistic appraisals of problems, recognizing and changing unhealthy emotional reactions, and trying to prevent adverse effects on the body. Maladaptive coping includes using alcohol or drugs to escape problems.

Stress and Disease

Chronic stress is linked to the development of many psychological problems, such as depression, anxiety, and schizophrenia. A large body of research also indicates that stress is linked to a variety of physical problems, including cancer, heart disease, rheumatoid arthritis, genital herpes, periodontal disease, yeast infections, and the common cold, to name just a few.

Stress and Immune Function

Stress affects the functioning of the immune system, as do age, nutrition, and genetic factors. The **immune system** is the body's defense against harmful agents such as bacteria, viruses, and other foreign substances. It communicates constantly with the brain and the endocrine system. Stress affects the immune system in many ways. For instance, hormones that are released in response to stress can inhibit the activity of lymphocytes.

Summary

Stress and Stressors

- Stress is defined differently by different researchers.
- One definition of stress is the experience of being threatened by taxing circumstances.
- Stress depends on how environmental events are appraised.
- Three types of stressors are catastrophic events, major life changes, and minor hassles.
- Stress is produced when people experience frustration, conflict, or pressure.
- Hans Selye proposed that the stress response consists of a general adaptation syndrome, which has three stages: alarm, resistance, and exhaustion.
- In stressful situations, the brain sends signals to the rest of the body along two pathways.

Coping

- Coping refers to efforts to manage stress.
- Coping can be adaptive or maladaptive.
- Adaptive coping involves direct confrontation of problems, realistic appraisals, recognizing and modifying unhealthy emotional reactions, and protecting bodily health.

- Maladaptive coping includes behaviors such as using alcohol and drugs to escape problems.

Stress and Disease

- Chronic stress is linked to the development of many psychological and physical problems.
- Stress can affect the immune system.

CHAPTER 11:
Psychological Disorders

When people think of mental illness, they often think of imaginary voices or terrifying killers like Charles Manson. However, psychological disorders are not always that dramatic—or that clear-cut. The question of what classifies as a mental disorder is often difficult to answer. Psychologists use many criteria to evaluate and diagnose these disorders, and they use a detailed system to classify them into categories. The origins of psychological disorders are varied and often unclear, and understanding these disorders involves an understanding of biology, culture, and personality.

What Is a Psychological Disorder?

Several criteria exist for defining a psychological disorder. Sometimes a person needs to meet only one criterion to be diagnosed as having a psychological disorder. In other cases, more than one of the following criteria may be met:

- Violation of cultural standards behavior
- Exhibition of behavior harmful to self or others
- Experiencing distress

Model of Psychological Disorders

Psychologists use different conceptual models for understanding, describing, and treating psychological disorders.

The Medical Model

The **medical model** is a way of describing and explaining psychological disorders as if they are diseases. Many terms used to discuss psychological disorders come from the medical model. **Diagnosis** refers to the process of distinguishing among disorders. **Etiology** refers to the cause or origin of a disorder. **_Prognosis_** refers to a prediction about the probable course and outcome of a disorder.

The Vulnerability-Stress Model
The **vulnerability-stress model** states that psychological disorders result from an interaction between biological and environmental factors. According to this model, individuals who have a biological vulnerability to a particular disorder will have the disorder only if certain environmental stressors are present.

The Learning Model
The **learning model** theorizes that psychological disorders result from the reinforcement of abnormal behavior.

The Psychodynamic Model
The **psychodynamic model** states that psychological disorders result from maladaptive defenses against unconscious conflicts.

Classification
Psychologists and psychiatrists have classified psychological disorders into categories. Classification allows clinicians and researchers to describe disorders, predict outcomes, consider treatments, and encourage research into their etiology.

The DSM
Psychologists and psychiatrists use a reference book called the **_Diagnostic and Statistical Manual of Mental Disorders_** (**DSM**) to diagnose psychological disorders. The American Psychiatric Association published the first version of the _DSM_ in 1952. It has been revised several times, and the newest version is commonly referred to as the _DSM-IV_.

The *DSM-IV* uses a multiaxial system of classification, which means that diagnoses are made on several different axes or dimensions. The *DSM* has five axes:

1. Axis I records the patient's primary diagnosis.
2. Axis II records long-standing personality problems or mental retardation.
3. Axis III records any medical conditions that might affect the patient psychologically.
4. Axis IV records any significant psychosocial or environmental problems experienced by the patient.
5. Axis V records an assessment of the patient's level of functioning.

Anxiety Disorders

Anxiety is a common and normal occurrence. However, a chronic high level of anxiety indicates an anxiety disorder.

Common Anxiety Disorders

Some of the more common anxiety disorders include:

- **Generalized anxiety disorder:** A person with **generalized anxiety disorder** experiences persistent and excessive anxiety or worry that lasts at least six months.
- **Specific phobia:** A person who has **specific phobia** experiences intense anxiety when exposed to a particular object or situation. The person often avoids the feared object or situation because of a desire to escape the anxiety associated with it.
- **Social phobia:** A person who has **social phobia** experiences intense anxiety when exposed to certain kinds of social or performance situations. As a result, the person often avoids these types of situations.
- **Panic disorder and agoraphobia:** A person with **panic disorder** experiences recurrent, unexpected panic attacks, which cause worry

or anxiety. During a **panic attack,** a person has symptoms such as heart palpitations, sweating, trembling, dizziness, chest pain, and fear of losing control, going crazy, or dying. Panic disorder can occur with or without agoraphobia. **Agoraphobia** involves anxiety about losing control in public places, being in situations from which escape would be difficult or embarrassing, or being in places where there might be no one to help if a panic attack occurred.

- **Obsessive-compulsive disorder:** A person with **obsessive-compulsive disorder** experiences obsessions, compulsions, or both. Obsessions are ideas, thoughts, impulses, or images that are persistent and cause anxiety or distress. A person usually feels that the obsessions are inappropriate but uncontrollable. **Compulsions** are repetitive behaviors that help to prevent or relieve anxiety.
- **Post-traumatic stress disorder (PTSD):** A person with this disorder persistently re-experiences a highly traumatic event and avoids stimuli associated with the trauma. Symptoms include increased arousal such as insomnia, irritability, difficulty concentrating, hypervigilance, or exaggerated startle response.

Roots of Anxiety Disorders
Many different interactive factors influence the development of anxiety disorders.

Biological Factors
Many biological factors can contribute to the onset of anxiety disorders:

- **Genetic predisposition:** Twin studies suggest that there may be genetic predispositions to anxiety disorders. Researchers typically use concordance rates to describe the likelihood that a disorder might be inherited. A **concordance rate** indicates the percentage of twin pairs who share a particular disorder. Research has shown that identical twins have a higher concordance rate for anxiety disorders than fraternal twins.

- **Differing sensitivity:** Some research suggests that people differ in sensitivity to anxiety. People who are highly sensitive to the physiological symptoms of anxiety react with even more anxiety to these symptoms, which sets off a worsening spiral of anxiety that can result in an anxiety disorder.
- **Neurotransmitters:** Researchers believe there is a link between anxiety disorders and disturbances in neural circuits that use the neurotransmitters GABA and serotonin. GABA limits nerve cell activity in the part of the brain associated with anxiety. People who do not produce enough GABA or whose brains do not process it normally may feel increased anxiety. Inefficient processing of serotonin may also contribute to anxiety.
- **Brain damage:** Some researchers have suggested that damage to the hippocampus can contribute to PTSD symptoms.

Conditioning and Learning

Research shows that conditioning and learning also play a role in anxiety disorders:

- **Classical conditioning:** People can acquire anxiety responses, especially phobias, through classical conditioning and then maintain them through operant conditioning. A neutral stimulus becomes associated with anxiety by being paired with an anxiety-producing stimulus. After this classical conditioning process has occurred, a person may begin to avoid the conditioned anxiety-producing stimulus. This leads to a decrease in anxiety, which reinforces the avoidance through an operant conditioning process.
- **Evolutionary predisposition:** Researchers such as **Martin Seligman** have proposed that people may be more likely to develop conditioned fears to certain objects and situations. According to this view, evolutionary history biologically prepares people to develop phobias about ancient dangers, such as snakes and heights.

- **Observational learning:** People also may develop phobias through observational learning. For example, children may learn to be afraid of certain objects or situations by observing their parents' behavior in the face of those objects or situations.

Cognitive Factors

Some researchers have suggested that people with certain styles of thinking are more susceptible to anxiety disorders than others. Such people have increased susceptibility for several reasons:

- They tend to see threats in harmless situations.
- They focus too much attention on situations that they perceive to be threatening.
- They tend to recall threatening information better than nonthreatening information.

Personality Traits

The personality trait of neuroticism is associated with a higher likelihood of having an anxiety disorder.

Mood Disorders

Mood disorders are characterized by marked disturbances in emotional state, which affect thinking, physical symptoms, social relationships, and behavior. If mood is viewed as a continuum, mood disorders occur when a person experiences moods that lie at either extreme of the continuum. Mood disorders are of two basic types: unipolar or bipolar. People with unipolar disorders experience moods that are at the depressive end of the continuum. People with bipolar disorders experience moods that are at both ends of the continuum.

Mood disorders are generally episodic, which means they tend to come and go. The duration of the disturbed emotional state and the pattern of its occurrence determine how a mood disorder is diagnosed.

Dysthymic Disorder

A person with **dysthymic disorder** experiences a depressed mood for a majority of days over at least two years.

Major Depressive Disorder

Major depressive disorder is characterized by at least one major depressive episode. A **major depressive episode** is a period of at least two weeks in which a person experiences some or all of the following symptoms:

- Constant sadness or irritability
- Loss of interest in almost all activities
- Changed sleeping or eating patterns
- Low energy
- Feelings of worthlessness or guilt
- Difficulty concentrating
- Recurrent thoughts about suicide

Major depressive disorder is much more common in women than in men.

Bipolar Disorders

Bipolar disorders involve at least one distinct period when a person exhibits manic symptoms. Manic symptoms include any or all of the following:

- Irritability
- Feelings of being high
- Decreased need for sleep
- Inflated self-esteem or grandiosity
- Fast and pressured speech
- Agitation
- Increased interest in pleasurable activities that have the potential for harmful consequences

People with bipolar disorders usually also experience major depressive episodes. Men and women are equally likely to suffer from bipolar disorders.

Etiology of Mood Disorders

Researchers believe that many different influences interact to produce mood disorders.

Biological Factors

Biological influences include the following:

- **Genetic predisposition:** Twin studies suggest that people can be genetically predisposed to major depressive disorder and bipolar disorders. Concordance rates for both major depressive disorder and bipolar disorders are higher for identical twins than fraternal twins. Genetic factors seem to be implicated more in depression among women than among men.
- **Neurotransmitters:** Research shows that the neurotransmitters norepinephrine and serotonin are involved in mood disorders.
- **Brain structure:** Some research indicates that people with chronic depression tend to have a smaller hippocampus and amygdala in the brain, perhaps because of an excess of the stress hormone cortisol.

Cognitive Factors

Many researchers have studied the various cognitive factors involved in depression:

- **Learned helplessness:** The psychologist **Martin Seligman** proposed that depression results from learned helplessness, or a tendency to give up passively in the face of unavoidable stressors. Seligman pointed out that people who have a pessimistic explanatory style are likely to experience depression.
- **Self-blame:** Depressed people tend to attribute negative events to internal, stable, and global factors. When a problem occurs, they blame

themselves rather than situational factors. They believe the problem is likely to be permanent, and they overgeneralize from the problem to their whole lives.

- **Low self-esteem:** Some researchers have suggested that a pessimistic worldview is only one of several factors that contribute to depression. They say that other factors such as low self-esteem and stress also play an important role. All these lead to hopelessness, which then leads to depression.

- **Rumination:** Rumination, or brooding about problems, is associated with longer periods of depression. Some researchers believe that women have higher rates of depression because they tend to ruminate more than men.

Interpersonal Factors

Various interpersonal influences are also linked to depression:

- **Lack of social network:** Depressed people tend to have less social support than other people, and the relationship between social support and depression is likely to be two-way. People with poor social skills may be more likely to develop depression. Once people are depressed, they tend to be unpleasant companions, which further reduces their social support.

- **Loss of an important relationship:** Some researchers have suggested that depression can result when people lose important relationships.

Environmental Stressors

The onset and course of mood disorders may be influenced by stress. Stress also affects people's responses to treatment and whether they are likely to have a relapse. Some researchers have suggested that women are more vulnerable to depression because they tend to experience more stress in the form of discrimination, poverty, and sexual abuse and because they may have less satisfying work and family lives than men.

Eating Disorders

Eating disorders are characterized by the following:

- Problematic eating patterns
- Extreme concerns about body weight
- Inappropriate behaviors aimed at controlling body weight

The two main types of eating disorders are anorexia nervosa and bulimia nervosa.

The large majority of eating disorders occur in females and are much more common in industrialized countries where people idealize thinness and have easy access to food. Eating disorders are also much more common in younger women.

Anorexia Nervosa

The main features of **anorexia nervosa** are a refusal to maintain a body weight in the normal range, intense fear about gaining weight, and highly distorted body image. In postpubescent women, another symptom of anorexia nervosa is absence of menstrual periods. Anorexia nervosa can result in serious medical problems, including anemia, kidney and cardiovascular malfunctions, dental problems, and osteoporosis.

Bulimia Nervosa

The main features of **bulimia nervosa** are habitual binge eating and unhealthy efforts to control body weight, including vomiting, fasting, excessive exercise, or use of laxatives, diuretics, and other medications. People with bulimia nervosa tend to evaluate themselves largely according to their body weight and shape. Unlike people with anorexia nervosa, people with bulimia nervosa typically have body weight in the normal range.

Bulimia nervosa can have serious medical consequences, including fluid and electrolyte imbalances and dental and gastrointestinal problems.

Etiology of Eating Disorders

Many different factors influence the development of eating disorders.

Biological Factors

Some evidence suggests a genetic vulnerability to eating disorders:

- Identical twins are more likely to both suffer from an eating disorder than are fraternal twins.
- Biological relatives of people with bulimia nervosa and anorexia nervosa appear to have an increased risk of developing the disorders.

Personality Factors

Some researchers have noted that people with eating disorders are more likely to have certain personality traits:

- People with anorexia nervosa tend to be obsessive, rigid, neurotic, and emotionally inhibited.
- People with bulimia nervosa tend to be impulsive and oversensitive and have poor self-esteem.

Cultural Factors

Cultural factors strongly influence the onset of eating disorders. One example is the high value placed on thinness in industrial countries.

Family Influences

Family environment may also influence the onset of eating disorders:

- Some theorists have suggested that eating disorders are related to insufficient autonomy within the family.
- Others have proposed that eating disorders might be affected by mothers who place too much emphasis on body weight.

Cognitive Factors

People with eating disorders show distortions of thinking, such as the tendency to think in rigid all-or-none terms. It is unclear whether this type of thinking causes the eating disorders or results from the eating disorders.

Stress

The onset of anorexia nervosa is often associated with stressful events such as leaving home for college.

Somatoform Disorders

Somatoform disorders are characterized by real physical symptoms that cannot be fully explained by a medical condition, the effects of a drug, or another mental disorder. People with somatoform disorders do not fake symptoms or produce symptoms intentionally.

Three common somatoform disorders are somatization disorder, conversion disorder, and hypochondriasis.

Somatization Disorder

Somatization disorder was formerly called hysteria or Briquet's syndrome. People with somatization disorder experience a wide variety of physical symptoms, such as pain and gastrointestinal, sexual, and pseudoneurological problems. The disorder usually affects women, begins before age thirty, and continues for many years.

Conversion Disorder

Conversion disorder is characterized by symptoms that affect voluntary motor functioning or sensory functioning. These symptoms cannot be explained medically. A conflict or other stressor precedes the onset or exacerbation of these symptoms, which implies a relationship between the symptoms and psychological factors.

Hypochondriasis

People with **hypochondriasis** are preoccupied with fears that they have a serious disease. They base these fears on misinterpretations of physical symptoms. People with this disorder continue to worry about having a serious medical problem even after they receive reassurances to the contrary. People with hypochondriasis, however, are not delusional—they can acknowledge that their worries might be excessive.

Etiology of Somatoform Disorders

Personality, cognitive factors, and learning appear to be involved in the etiology of somatoform disorders.

Personality Factors

Some researchers have suggested that people with histrionic personality traits are more likely to develop somatoform disorders. **Histrionic** people enjoy being the center of attention. They tend to be self-focused, excitable, highly open to suggestion, very emotional, and dramatic.

Cognitive Factors

Researchers have proposed that several cognitive factors contribute to somatoform disorders:

- People with these disorders may pay too much attention to bodily sensations.
- They may make catastrophic conclusions when they experience minor symptoms.
- They may have distorted ideas about good health and expect healthy people to be free of any symptoms or discomfort.

Learning

People with somatoform disorders may learn to adopt a sick role because they are reinforced for being sick. Rewards that help to maintain sickness include attention and sympathy from others and avoidance of work and family challenges.

Substance-Related Disorders

The *DSM* describes many substance-related disorders, which occur when a person is intoxicated by, withdrawing from, using, abusing, or dependent on one or more drugs. Two common types of substance-related disorders are substance abuse and substance dependence.

Substance Abuse

The *DSM* defines **substance abuse** as a maladaptive pattern of drug use that results in repeated negative consequences such as legal, social, work-related, or school-related problems. A drug abuser may even use drugs in situations in which it is physically dangerous to do so.

Substance Dependence

Substance dependence, or drug addiction, involves continuing to use a drug despite persistent physical or psychological costs. A person who is addicted to drugs may make several unsuccessful attempts to give up the drug and may even develop tolerance for the drug. **Tolerance** is the gradual need for more and more of the drug to get the same effect. The person may also experience **withdrawal symptoms** such as sweating, nausea, muscle pain, shakiness, and irritability when he or she stops taking the drug.

Etiology of Substance Dependence

Many researchers believe biology and environment interact to produce substance dependence.

Biological Influences

Several lines of research have examined genetic predispositions to drug dependence. Researchers think there may be a genetic predisposition to one particular type of alcoholism: the type that begins in adolescence and that is associated with impulsive, antisocial, and criminal behavior. With other types of alcoholism, many genes may interact to play a role.

Genes may influence traits such as impulsivity, which can make a person more likely to become alcoholic. Genes may also influence the level of dopamine in the brain. Researchers have suggested that high dopamine levels may in turn influence the susceptibility to alcoholism.

Just as biological factors may make a person susceptible to dependence, heavy use of drugs can affect a person's biological makeup. For example, excessive drug use can reduce the number of dopamine receptors in the brain. Since dopamine is involved in feeling pleasure, the reduced number of receptors can then make a person dependent on the drug. The person will crave more of the drug in order to feel the same amount of pleasure.

Environmental Influences

Research findings suggest that certain environmental factors play a key role in substance dependence:

- **Cultural norms:** The pattern of drug dependence varies according to cultural norms. For example, alcohol dependence is rarer in countries where children learn to drink responsibly and in moderation and where excessive drinking by adults is considered improper. Alcohol dependence is more common in societies that condone adult drunkenness and forbid children to drink.
- **Social policy:** Governmental policies that totally prohibit alcohol consumption tend to increase rates of alcohol dependence.
- **Variation in symptoms:** The existence of withdrawal symptoms after discontinuing a drug depends on many factors, including a person's expectations and context. This suggests that dependence is not just a biological phenomenon.
- **Reasons for drug use**: A person's tendency toward drug addiction depends not only on the properties of the drug but also on the reasons

a person uses the drug. For example, people who receive prescription narcotics in hospitals for postsurgical pain may not become addicted, while others who use narcotics to escape stress may become addicted.

Schizophrenia

Schizophrenia is one of several psychotic disorders described in the *DSM*. People with psychotic disorders lose contact with reality and often have delusions or hallucinations. People with schizophrenia have a wide range of symptoms, which can be classified into positive or negative symptoms.

Positive Symptoms

Positive symptoms involve the presence of altered behaviors. Examples of positive symptoms include delusions, hallucinations, disorganized speech, and disorganized behavior. **Delusions** are false beliefs that are strongly held despite contradictory evidence. Hallucinations are sensory or perceptual experiences that happen without any external stimulus. **Hallucinations** can occur in any sensory modality, but auditory hallucinations are most common in schizophrenia. Disorganized speech can also take many forms. For example, a person with schizophrenia may produce word salad, which consists of words and sentences strung together in an incoherent way. Examples of disorganized behavior include inappropriate gestures or laughter, agitated pacing, or unpredictable violence.

Negative Symptoms

Negative symptoms involve an absence or reduction of normal behavior. Negative symptoms include emotional flatness, social withdrawal, spare or uninflected speech, and lack of motivation.

Subtypes of Schizophrenia

Schizophrenia is classified into four subtypes, depending on the symptoms present at the time of evaluation:

1. **Paranoid type:** Characterized by marked delusions or hallucinations and relatively normal cognitive and emotional functioning. Delusions are usually persecutory, grandiose, or both. **Persecutory delusions** involve a belief that one is being oppressed, pursued, or harassed in some way. **Grandiose delusions** involve the belief that one is very important or famous. This subtype usually happens later in life than the other subtypes. Prognosis may also be better for this subtype than for other subtypes.

2. **Disorganized type:** Characterized by disorganized behavior, disorganized speech, and emotional flatness or inappropriateness.

3. **Catatonic type:** Characterized by unnatural movement patterns such as rigid, unmoving posture or continual, purposeless movements, or by unnatural speech patterns such as absence of speech or parroting of other people's speech.

4. **Undifferentiated type:** Diagnosis given to a patient that does not meet criteria for paranoid, disorganized, or catatonic schizophrenia.

Etiology of Schizophrenia

As with other psychological disorders, researchers have studied the etiology of schizophrenia from different perspectives.

Biological Factors

Research suggests that genes, neurotransmitters, and brain abnormalities play a role in the onset of schizophrenia:

- **Genetic predisposition:** Substantial evidence suggests that there is a genetically inherited predisposition to schizophrenia. For example, there is a concordance rate of about 48 percent for identical twins. The concordance rate for fraternal twins is considerably less, about 17 percent. **Concordance rate** refers to the percentage of both people in a pair having a certain trait or disorder. A person who has two parents with schizophrenia has about a 46 percent chance of developing schizophrenia. This probability is very high compared to the roughly 1 percent chance of developing schizophrenia in the general population.

- **Neurotransmitters:** Some researchers have proposed that schizophrenia is related to an overabundance of the neurotransmitter dopamine in the brain. Other researchers have suggested that both serotonin and dopamine may be implicated. The neurotransmitter glutamate may also play a role in the disorder. Underdevelopment of glutamate neurons results in the overactivity of dopamine neurons.
- **Brain structure:** Some researchers have suggested that schizophrenia may involve an inability to filter out irrelevant information, which leads to being overwhelmed by stimuli. With this idea in mind, researchers have looked for brain abnormalities in schizophrenia patients. The brains of people with schizophrenia do differ structurally from the brains of normal people in several ways. For example, they are more likely to have enlarged ventricles, or fluid-filled spaces. They are also more likely to have abnormalities in the thalamus and reduced hippocampus volume.
- **Brain injury:** Another line of research suggests that injuries to the brain during sensitive periods of development can make people susceptible to schizophrenia later on in life. For example, researchers believe that viral infections or malnutrition during the prenatal period and complications during the birthing process can increase the later risk of schizophrenia. Some researchers have suggested that abnormal brain development during adolescence may also play a role in schizophrenia.

Stress

Many researchers believe stress plays a role in bringing on schizophrenia in people who are already biologically vulnerable to this disorder.

Dissociative Disorders

Dissociative disorders are characterized by disturbances in consciousness, memory, identity, and perception.

Three kinds of dissociative disorders are dissociative amnesia, dissociative fugue, and dissociative identity disorder.

Dissociative Amnesia

The main feature of **dissociative amnesia** is an inability to remember important personal information, usually about something traumatic or painful. The memory loss is too extensive to be explained by normal forgetfulness.

Dissociative Fugue

People with **dissociative fugue** suddenly leave their homes and disappear unexpectedly. They do not remember their past and are confused about their identity. Sometimes, they may assume entirely new identities.

Dissociative Identity Disorder

Dissociative identity disorder was formerly called multiple personality disorder. In this disorder, certain aspects of identity, consciousness, and memory are not integrated. People with dissociative identity disorder cannot remember important personal information and have two or more identities or personality states that control their behavior. Often, each of these identities has a separate name, personal history, set of characteristics, and self-image.

Etiology of Dissociative Disorders

Many researchers believe that severe stress plays a role in the onset of dissociative disorders. However, they cannot explain why only a small minority of people who experience severe stress develop such disorders.

Personality Disorders

Personality disorders are stable patterns of experience and behavior that differ noticeably from patterns that are considered normal by a person's culture. Symptoms of a personality disorder remain the same across different situations and manifest by early adulthood. These symptoms cause distress or make it difficult for a person to function normally in society.

- **Schizoid personality disorder:** entails social withdrawal and restricted expression of emotions
- **Borderline personality disorder:** characterized by impulsive behavior and unstable relationships, emotions, and self-image
- **Histrionic personality disorder:** involves attention-seeking behavior and shallow emotions
- **Narcissistic personality disorder:** characterized by an exaggerated sense of importance, a strong desire to be admired, and a lack of empathy
- **Avoidant personality disorder:** includes social withdrawal, low self-esteem, and extreme sensitivity to negative evaluation
- **Antisocial personality disorder:** characterized by a lack of respect for other people's rights, feelings, and needs, beginning by age fifteen. People with antisocial personality disorder are deceitful and manipulative and tend to break the law frequently. They often lack empathy and remorse but can be superficially charming. Their behavior is often aggressive, impulsive, reckless, and irresponsible. Antisocial personality disorder has been referred to in the past as sociopathy or psychopathy.

Etiology of Antisocial Personality Disorder (APD)

Researchers have proposed that the following biological factors might be related to the etiology of antisocial personality disorder:

- People with this disorder may have central nervous system abnormalities that prevent them from experiencing anxiety in stressful situations. Because they feel no anxiety, they never learn to avoid behavior with negative consequences.

- Such people may also have a genetically inherited inability to control impulses.
- Some researchers have suggested that antisocial personality disorder may be caused by brain damage. Injuries to the prefrontal cortex, which is involved in planning and impulse control, may be particularly involved.

As with other disorders, however, biological factors alone are often not enough to cause APD. Environmental factors, such as family abuse or dysfunction, also play a large role in the development of APD. Generally, it is the combination of these environmental factors with the biological vulnerability that brings on the disorder.

Summary

What Is a Psychological Disorder?
- Criteria for defining psychological disorders depend on whether cultural norms are violated, whether behavior is maladaptive or harmful, and whether there is distress.
- The medical model describes and explains psychological disorders as if they are diseases.
- The vulnerability-stress model states that disorders are caused by an interaction between biological and environmental factors.
- The learning model theorizes that psychological disorders result from the reinforcement of abnormal behavior.
- The psychodynamic model states that psychological disorders result from maladaptive defenses against unconscious conflicts.
- Psychologists use objective and projective tests to assess psychological disorders.

Classification
- Classification allows psychologists to describe disorders, predict outcomes, consider treatments, and study etiology.
- Psychologists and psychiatrists use the *DSM* to diagnose psychological disorders.
- The DSM uses a multi-axial system of classification.

Anxiety Disorders
- A chronic, high level of anxiety may be a sign of an anxiety disorder.
- Generalized anxiety disorder involves persistent and excessive anxiety for at least six months.
- Having a specific phobia means becoming anxious when exposed to a specific circumstance.
- Social phobia is characterized by anxiety in social or performance situations.
- A person with panic disorder experiences recurrent, unexpected panic attacks.
- Agoraphobia involves anxiety about having panic attacks in difficult or embarrassing situations.
- Obsessive-compulsive disorder entails obsessions, compulsions, or both.
- Post–traumatic stress disorder is a set of psychological and physiological responses to a highly traumatic event.
- Biological factors implicated in the onset of anxiety disorders include genes, different sensitivity to anxiety, the neurotransmitters GABA and serotonin, and brain damage.
- Conditioning and learning may contribute to the development of phobias.
- Some styles of thinking may make people more susceptible to anxiety disorders.
- Neuroticism is associated with anxiety disorders.

Mood Disorders

- Mood disorders are characterized by marked disturbances in emotional state, which cause physical symptoms and affect thinking, social relationships, and behavior.
- Mood disorders may be unipolar or bipolar.
- People with dysthymic disorder have depressed mood for at least two years.
- Major depressive disorder involves at least one period with significant depressive symptoms.
- Bipolar disorders involve at least one period with manic symptoms and usually depressive periods as well.
- Biological influences on mood disorders include genes, the neurotransmitters norepinephrine and serotonin, and brain abnormalities.
- There is a two-way relationship between negative thinking and depression.
- Cognitive characteristics of depressed people include learned helplessness; a pessimistic worldview; hopelessness; a tendency to make internal, stable, global attributions; and a tendency to ruminate.
- There is a two-way relationship between social support and depression.
- Depression may be related to experiences of loss.
- The onset and course of mood disorders may be influenced by stress.

Eating Disorders

- Eating disorders are characterized by problematic eating patterns, concerns about body weight, and inappropriate efforts to control weight.
- Anorexia nervosa entails very low body weight, fear of gaining weight, and distorted body image.
- Bulimia nervosa involves binge eating and unhealthy efforts to control body weight.

- Some people may have a genetic vulnerability to eating disorders.
- Eating disorders may be associated with particular personality traits.
- Cultural factors strongly influence the onset of eating disorders.
- Lacking autonomy in the family and having an overly weight-conscious mother may influence the onset of eating disorders.
- People with eating disorders tend to have certain distortions of thinking.
- The onset of anorexia nervosa may be associated with stressful events.

Somatoform Disorders

- Somatoform disorders are characterized by real physical symptoms that cannot be fully explained by a medical condition, the effects of a drug, or another mental disorder.
- A person with somatization disorder has many different, recurrent physical symptoms.
- Conversion disorder involves symptoms that affect voluntary motor functioning or sensory functioning.
- People with hypochondriasis constantly fear that they may have a serious disease.
- People with histrionic personality traits may be more likely to develop somatoform disorders.
- Several cognitive factors may contribute to somatoform disorders.
- People with somatoform disorders may learn to adopt a sick role.

Substance-Related Disorders

- Many substance-related disorders are described in the DSM.
- Substance abuse is a maladaptive pattern of drug use that results in repeated, negative legal, social, occupational, or academic consequences.
- Substance dependence involves continuing to use a drug despite persistent harmful physical or psychological consequences.
- The disease model of addiction holds that addiction is a disease that must be treated medically.

- The learning model of addiction holds that addiction is a way of coping with stress.
- Genes may produce a predisposition to substance dependence.
- Several lines of evidence suggest that environmental factors play a key role in substance dependence.

Schizophrenia

- Schizophrenia is a psychotic disorder that includes positive and negative symptoms. There are several subtypes of schizophrenia.
- The paranoid type is characterized by marked delusions or hallucinations and relatively normal cognitive and emotional functioning.
- The disorganized type involves disorganized behavior, disorganized speech, and emotional flatness or inappropriateness.
- The catatonic type is characterized by unnatural movement or speech patterns.
- A diagnosis of undifferentiated type applies if diagnostic criteria are not met for any of the above three subtypes.
- Research suggests that genes, neurotransmitters, and brain abnormalities are involved in the onset of schizophrenia.
- Stress may help to induce schizophrenia in people who are already biologically vulnerable to the disorder.

Dissociative Disorders

- Dissociative disorders are characterized by disturbances in consciousness, memory, identity, and perception.
- Dissociative fugue involves sudden and unexpected travel away from home, failure to remember the past, and confusion about identity.
- People with dissociative identity disorder fail to remember important personal information and have two or more identities or personality states that control behavior.
- Severe stress may play a role in the onset of dissociative disorders.

Personality Disorders

- Personality disorders are stable patterns of experience and behavior that differ noticeably from patterns that are considered normal by a person's culture.
- People with schizoid personality disorder are socially withdrawn and have restricted expression of emotions.
- Borderline personality disorder involves impulsive behavior and unstable relationships, emotions, and self-image.
- Histrionic personality disorder is characterized by attention-seeking behavior and shallow emotions.
- People with narcissistic personality disorder have an exaggerated sense of importance, a strong desire to be admired, and a lack of empathy.
- Avoidant personality disorder involves social withdrawal, low self-esteem, and extreme sensitivity to being evaluated negatively.
- Antisocial personality disorder begins by age fifteen and includes a lack of respect for other people's rights, feelings, and needs.
- Abnormalities in physiological arousal, a genetically inherited inability to control impulses, and brain damage may be involved in the development of antisocial personality disorder.
- Environmental influences are also likely to influence the development of antisocial personality disorder.

CHAPTER 12:
Psychological Treatment

Cartoon characterizations of psychological treatment typically involve a client lying tensely on a couch while a poker-faced therapist sits nearby, taking notes. Real treatments for psychological problems rarely fit this image. Hundreds of different treatments exist, including medication, electric shock, and surgery. Some types involve unorthodox and often strange procedures, such as making rapid eye movements.

Talk therapy is another common type of treatment. Therapists vary in their style and approach from client to client, and although some therapists still have their clients lie on couches, most therapists sit face-to-face with them. Some therapists take a relatively passive, listening role in therapy sessions, while others actively discuss problems or even argue with clients. All these treatments have different rationales and varying degrees of success. The type of treatment used and the effectiveness of that treatment sometimes depend as much on the client as on the treatment itself.

Types of Treatment

There are many different types of treatment for psychological disorders, all of which fit into three broad types: insight therapies, behavior therapies, and biomedical therapies.

Insight therapies involve complex conversations between therapists and clients. The aim is to help clients understand the nature of their problems and the meaning of their behaviors, thoughts, and feelings. Insight therapists may use a variety of approaches, including psychodynamic, cognitive, or humanistic.

Behavior therapies also involve conversations between therapists and clients but attempt to directly influence maladaptive behaviors. Behavior therapies are based on learning principles. (See Chapter 3 for more information on learning.)

Biomedical therapies involve efforts to directly alter biological functioning through medication, electric shock, or surgery.

Psychotherapy

Psychotherapy is the treatment of psychological problems through confidential verbal communications with a mental health professional. All psychotherapies offer hope that a problem will improve, present new perspectives on the problem, and encourage an empathic relationship with a therapist. The approach a psychotherapist uses depends on his or her theoretical orientation.

Psychodynamic Approaches

All of the many psychodynamic therapies derive from the treatment called *psychoanalysis*, which Sigmund Freud developed and used in the late 1800s and early 1900s. Psychoanalytic treatment focuses on uncovering unconscious motives, conflicts, and defenses that relate to childhood experiences. Freud believed that people experience anxiety because of conflicts among the **id, ego,** and **superego**. To manage these conflicts, people use defense mechanisms, which can often be self-defeating and unsuccessful at fully controlling anxiety.

Psychoanalytic Techniques

In the traditional form of psychoanalysis, clients meet with a psychoanalyst several times a week for many years. The psychoanalyst sits out of view of the client, who sometimes lies on a couch. Some techniques commonly used in psychoanalysis include free association, dream analysis, and interpretation:

- **Free association:** Psychoanalysts encourage clients to say anything that comes to mind. Clients are expected to put all thoughts into words, even if those thoughts are incoherent, inappropriate, rude, or seemingly irrelevant. Free associations reveal the client's unconscious to the psychoanalyst.

- **Dream analysis:** Dreams also reveal the subconscious. Clients describe their dreams in detail, and the psychoanalyst interprets the latent content, or the hidden meaning, of these dreams.
- **Interpretation:** A key technique in psychoanalysis, interpretation refers to the psychoanalyst's efforts to uncover the hidden meanings in the client's free associations, dreams, feelings, memories, and behavior. Psychoanalysts are trained to make interpretations carefully and only when a client is ready to accept them. Ideally, such interpretations increase the client's insight.

Psychoanalytic Concepts

Three important concepts involved in psychoanalysis are transference, resistance, and catharsis:

- **Transference** refers to the process by which clients relate to their psychoanalysts as they would to important figures in their past. Psychoanalysts usually encourage transference because it helps them to uncover the client's hidden conflicts and helps the client to work through such conflicts.
- **Resistance** refers to the client's efforts to block the progress of treatment. These efforts are usually unconscious. Resistance occurs because the client experiences anxiety when unconscious conflicts begin to be uncovered.
- **Catharsis** is the release of tension that results when repressed thoughts or memories move into the patient's conscious mind.

Current Psychodynamic Therapies

Today, the classical form of psychoanalysis is rarely practiced. Psychodynamic therapies, however, are widely used for treating the full range of psychological disorders. Psychodynamic therapies differ in their specific approaches, but they all focus on increasing insight by uncovering unconscious motives, conflicts, and defenses.

Interpretation and the concepts of transference and resistance are important features of psychodynamic therapies. Unlike traditional psychoanalysts, psychodynamic therapists usually sit face-to-face with their clients. Sessions typically occur once or twice a week, and treatment usually does not last as long as psychoanalysis.

Cognitive Approaches

Cognitive therapies aim to identify and change maladaptive thinking patterns that can result in negative emotions and dysfunctional behavior. Psychologist **Aaron Beck** first developed cognitive therapy to treat depression, although cognitive therapies are now used to treat a wide range of disorders. Beck's cognitive therapy helps clients test whether their beliefs are realistic.

Cognitive therapists such as Beck believe that depression arises from errors in thinking. According to this theory, depressed people tend to do any of the following:

- Blame themselves for negative events. They underestimate situational causes.
- Pay more attention to negative events than to positive ones.
- Be pessimistic.
- Make inappropriately global generalizations from negative events.

Cognitive Therapy Techniques

Cognitive therapists try to change their clients' ways of thinking. In therapy, clients learn to identify automatic negative thoughts and the assumptions they make about the world. **Automatic thoughts** are self-defeating judgments that people make about themselves. Clients learn to see these judgments as unrealistic and to consider other interpretations for events they encounter.

Behavioral Approaches

Whereas insight therapies focus on addressing the problems that underlie symptoms, behavior therapists focus on addressing symptoms, which they believe are the real problem. Behavior therapies use learning principles to modify maladaptive behaviors. Many therapists combine behavior therapy and cognitive therapy into an approach known as cognitive-behavior therapy.

Behavior therapies are based on two assumptions:

- Behavior is learned.
- Behavior can be changed by applying the principles of classical conditioning, operant conditioning, and observational learning.

Behavior therapies are designed for specific types of problems. Three important types of behavior therapies are systematic desensitization, aversion therapy, and social skills training.

Systematic Desensitization

Systematic desensitization is a treatment designed by the psychologist **Joseph Wolpe**. It uses counterconditioning to decrease anxiety symptoms. This therapy works on the assumption that anxiety arises through classical conditioning. That is, a neutral stimulus begins to arouse anxiety when it is paired with an unconditioned stimulus that evokes anxiety.

Systematic desensitization aims to replace the conditioned stimulus with a response, such as relaxation, that is incompatible with anxiety. If psychotherapists can teach their clients to relax whenever they encounter an anxiety-producing stimulus, the anxiety will gradually decrease.

Aversion Therapy

In **aversion therapy**, a stimulus that evokes an unpleasant response is paired with a stimulus that evokes a maladaptive behavior.

Therapists use aversion therapy to treat problems such as deviant sexual behavior, substance abuse, and overeating. One major limitation of this type of therapy is that people know that the aversive stimulus occurs only during therapy sessions. Aversion therapy is usually used in combination with other treatments.

Social Skills Training

Social skills training aims to enhance a client's relationships with other people. Techniques used in social skills training include modeling, behavioral rehearsal, and shaping:

- **Modeling** involves having clients learn specific skills by observing socially skilled people.
- **Behavioral rehearsal** involves having the client role-play behavior that could be used in social situations. The therapist provides feedback about the client's behavior.
- **Shaping** involves having the client approach progressively more difficult social situations in the real world.

Humanistic Approaches

Humanistic therapies are derived from the school of humanistic psychology. Humanistic therapists try to help people accept themselves and free themselves from unnecessary limitations. The influence of humanistic therapies led to the use of the term *clients*, rather than *patients*, in referring to people who seek therapy. Humanistic therapists tend to focus on the present situation of clients rather than their past. The best-known humanistic therapy is client-centered therapy.

Client-Centered Therapy

Client-centered, or person-centered, **therapy** was developed by **Carl Rogers**. It aims to help clients enhance self-acceptance and personal growth by providing a supportive emotional environment. This type of therapy is nondirective, which means that the therapist does not direct the course and pace of therapy. Client-centered therapists believe that people's problems come from **incongruence**, or a disparity between their self-concept and reality. Incongruence arises because people are too dependent on others for approval and acceptance. When people have incongruence, they feel anxious. They subsequently try to maintain their self-concept by denying or distorting reality.

In client-centered therapy, people learn to adopt a more realistic self-concept by accepting who they are and thus becoming less reliant on the acceptance of others.

Family Therapies

In **family therapy**, a therapist sees two or more members of a family at the same time. Family therapies work on the assumption that people do not live in isolation but as interconnected members of families. A problem that affects one person in the family must necessarily affect the whole family, and any change a person makes will inevitably affect the whole family. Family therapists help people to identify the roles they play in their families and to resolve conflicts within families. Family therapists sometimes use family trees to help family members identify intergenerational patterns of behavior.

In **couples therapy**, therapists help couples identify and resolve conflicts. Therapists usually see both members of a couple at the same time. Family and couples therapists may use psychodynamic, cognitive, behavioral, or humanistic approaches.

Group Therapies

In group therapy, a therapist meets with several people at once. Psychotherapy groups usually have between four and fifteen people. Group therapies are cost-effective for clients and time-saving for therapists.

Biomedical Therapies

Biomedical therapies include drug therapy, electroconvulsive therapy, and psychosurgery.

Drug Therapies

Drug therapy, or **psychopharmacotherapy**, aims to treat psychological disorders with medications. Drug therapy is usually combined with other kinds of psychotherapy. The main categories of drugs used to treat psychological disorders are antianxiety drugs, antidepressants, and antipsychotics.

Antianxiety Drugs

Antianxiety drugs include a class of drugs called **benzodiazepines**, or tranquilizers. Two commonly used benzodiazepines are known by the brand names Valium and Xanax. The generic names of these drugs are diazepam and alprazolam, respectively.

- **Effects:** Benzodiazepines reduce the activity of the central nervous system by increasing the activity of GABA, the main inhibitory neurotransmitter in the brain. Benzodiazepines take effect almost immediately after they are administered, but their effects last just a few hours. Psychiatrists prescribe these drugs for panic disorder and anxiety.

- **Side effects:** Side effects may include drowsiness, light-headedness, dry mouth, depression, nausea and vomiting, constipation, insomnia, confusion, diarrhea, palpitations, nasal congestion, and blurred vision. Benzodiazepines can also cause drug dependence. Tolerance can occur if a person takes these drugs for a long time, and withdrawal symptoms often appear when the drug use is discontinued.

Antidepressant Drugs

Antidepressants usually take a few weeks to have an effect. There are three classes of antidepressants: monoamine oxidase inhibitors, tricyclics, and selective serotonin reuptake inhibitors.

- **Monoamine oxidase inhibitors (MAOIs):** Include phenelzine (Nardil).
- **Tricyclics:** Include amitriptyline (Elavil). Tricyclics generally have fewer side effects than the MAOIs.

- **Selective serotonin reuptake inhibitors (SSRIs):** The newest class of antidepressants, including paroxetine (Paxil), fluoxetine (Prozac), and sertraline (Zoloft).

Antidepressants are typically prescribed for depression, anxiety, phobias, and obsessive-compulsive disorder.

- **Effects:** MAOIs and tricyclics increase the level of the neurotransmitters norepinephrine and serotonin in the brain. SSRIs increase the level of serotonin.
- **Side effects:** Although antidepressants are not addictive, they often have side effects such as headache, dry mouth, constipation, nausea, weight gain, and feelings of restlessness. Of the three classes of antidepressants, MAOIs generally have the most side effects. People who take MAOIs also have to restrict their diet, because MAOIs interact negatively with foods that contain the amino acid tyramine, such as beer and some cheeses and meats. SSRIs have fewer side effects than the other two classes of antidepressants. However, SSRIs can cause sexual dysfunction, and if they are discontinued abruptly, withdrawal symptoms occur.

Antipsychotic Drugs

Antipsychotic drugs are used to treat schizophrenia and other psychotic disorders. They include chlorpromazine (Thorazine), thioridazine (Mellaril), and haloperidol (Haldol). Antipsychotic drugs usually begin to take effect a few days after they are administered.

- **Effects:** Antipsychotic drugs, or neuroleptics, reduce sensitivity to irrelevant stimuli by limiting the activity of the neurotransmitter dopamine. Many antipsychotic drugs are most useful for treating positive symptoms of schizophrenia, such as hallucinations and delusions. However, a new class of antipsychotic drugs, called atypical antipsychotic drugs, also help treat the negative symptoms of schizophrenia. They reduce the activity of both dopamine and serotonin. Atypical antipsychotic drugs include clozapine (Clozaril), olanzapine (Zyprexa), and quetiapine (Seroquel). Atypical antipsychotic drugs can sometimes be effective for schizophrenia patients who have not responded to the older antipsychotic drugs.

- **Side effects:** Side effects include drowsiness, constipation, dry mouth, tremors, muscle rigidity, and coordination problems. These side effects often make people stop taking the medications, which frequently results in a relapse of schizophrenia. A more serious side effect is tardive dyskinesia, a usually permanent neurological condition characterized by involuntary movements. To avoid tardive dyskinesia, the dosage of antipsychotics has to be carefully monitored. The atypical antipsychotics have fewer side effects than the older antipsychotic drugs and are less likely to cause tardive dyskinesia. In addition, relapse rates are lower if people continue to take the drug. However, the relapse rate is higher with these drugs if people discontinue the drug.

Electroconvulsive Therapy

Electroconvulsive therapy (ECT) is used mainly for the treatment of severe depression. Electrodes are placed on the patient's head, over the temporal lobes of the brain. Anesthetics and muscle relaxants help minimize discomfort to the patient. Then an electric current is delivered for about one second. The patient has a convulsive seizure and becomes unconscious, awakening after about an hour. The typical number of ECT sessions varies from six to twenty, and they are usually done while a patient is hospitalized.

ECT is a controversial procedure. Research suggests that there are short-term side effects of ECT, such as attention deficits and memory loss. Critics of ECT believe that it is often used inappropriately and that it can result in permanent cognitive problems. Proponents of ECT, however, believe that it does not cause long-term cognitive problems, loss of memory, or brain damage. They believe that it is highly effective and that it is underused because of negative public ideas surrounding it.

Psychosurgery

Psychosurgery is brain surgery to treat a psychological disorder. The best-known form of psychosurgery is the prefrontal lobotomy. A **lobotomy** is a surgical procedure that severs nerve tracts in the frontal lobe. Surgeons performed lobotomies in the 1940s and 1950s to treat highly emotional and violent behavior. The surgery often resulted in severe deficits, including apathy, lethargy, and social withdrawal.

Lobotomies are now rarely performed, but some neurosurgeons perform **cingulotomies**, which involve destruction of part of the frontal lobes. These surgeries are usually performed on patients who have severe depressive or anxiety disorders and who do not respond to other treatments. The effectiveness of these surgeries is unclear.

Transcranial Magnetic Stimulation

Transcranial magnetic stimulation (TMS) is a recently developed, noninvasive procedure. It involves stimulating the brain by means of a magnetic coil held to a person's skull near the left prefrontal cortex. It is used to treat severe depression.

Summary

Types of Treatment

- Treatment for psychological disorders can be categorized into insight therapies, behavior therapies, and biomedical therapies.
- All psychotherapies offer hope, new perspectives on a problem, and an empathic relationship with a therapist.
- Many types of professionals provide psychological treatment.

Psychotherapy

- All psychodynamic therapies are based on Sigmund Freud's psychoanalytic treatment.
- Psychoanalytic treatment focuses on uncovering unconscious motives, conflicts, and defenses.
- Three techniques used in psychoanalysis are free association, dream analysis, and interpretation.
- The concepts of transference and resistance are important features of psychoanalysis and current psychodynamic therapies.
- Cognitive therapies attempt to identify and change maladaptive thinking patterns.
- Cognitive therapists believe that depression arises from errors in thinking.
- Cognitive therapists help clients to identify and change automatic thoughts and assumptions about the world.
- Behavior therapists focus on addressing symptoms rather than the underlying causes. They use learning principles to modify behavior.
- Systematic desensitization is a type of exposure therapy that uses counterconditioning to decrease anxiety. It is effective at treating phobias.
- In aversion therapy, a stimulus that evokes an unpleasant response is paired with a stimulus that evokes a maladaptive behavior.
- Social skills training for improving relationships with people uses techniques such as modeling, behavioral rehearsal, and shaping.
- Humanistic therapists try to help people accept themselves and free themselves from unnecessary limitations.
- In client-centered therapy, therapists provide a supportive emotional environment that helps clients enhance self-acceptance and personal growth.
- Humanistic therapists believe that it is important to be genuine and empathic and provide unconditional positive regard.

Family Therapies

- In family therapy, a therapist sees two or more members of a family at the same time. Family therapies are based on the idea that people live as interconnected members of families.
- In couples therapy, therapists help couples to identify and resolve conflicts.

Biomedical Therapies

- In drug therapy, psychological disorders are treated with medications. These medications are often effective but have many side effects.
- Antianxiety drugs include benzodiazepines, which reduce central nervous system activity.
- Antidepressants include MAOIs, tricyclics, and SSRIs. These drugs affect the levels of the neurotransmitters serotonin and epinephrine.
- Antipsychotic drugs are used to treat schizophrenia and other psychotic drugs. They reduce dopamine activity.
- Unlike the older antipsychotic drugs, the newer atypical antipsychotic drugs help treat the negative symptoms of schizophrenia. These drugs reduce serotonin activity as well as dopamine.
- ECT is used to treat severe depression. It is a controversial procedure.
- Lobotomies are performed only rarely to treat psychological disorders, but cingulotomies are sometimes done.
- TMS is a recently developed noninvasive procedure for treating severe depression.

CHAPTER 13:
Social Psychology

Social psychologists try to explain how other people influence our thoughts, feelings, and behavior; how we form impressions of other people; and why stereotypes and prejudice flourish. They study how people manage to persuade, influence, and attract us. Obedience to authorities, group functioning, and helpfulness are part of social psychology as well. Social psychology acknowledges that we move in and out of one another's lives, directly and indirectly, and all parties are, in some way, affected.

Impressions

People form impressions, or vague ideas, about other people through the process of **person perception**.

The Influence of Physical Appearance

Physical appearance has a strong effect on how people are perceived by others. Two aspects of physical appearance are particularly important: attractiveness and baby-faced features.

Attractiveness

Research shows that people judge attractive-looking people as having positive personality traits, such as sociability, friendliness, poise, warmth, and good adjustment. There is, however, little actual correlation between personality traits and physical attractiveness.

People also tend to think that attractive-looking people are more competent. Because of this bias, attractive people tend to get better jobs and higher salaries.

Baby-Faced Features

People's attractiveness does not have much influence on judgments about their honesty. Instead, people tend to be judged as honest if they have baby-faced features, such as large eyes and rounded chins. Baby-faced people are often judged as being passive, helpless, and naïve. However, no correlation exists between being baby-faced and actually having these personality traits.

Cognitive Schemas

When people meet, they form impressions of each other based on their **cognitive schemas**. People use cognitive schemas to organize information about the world. Cognitive schemas help to access information quickly and easily.

Social schemas are mental models that represent and categorize social events and people. For example, certain social schemas tell people what it means to be a spectator at a baseball game. There are also social schemas for categories of people, such as *yuppie* or *geek*. These social schemas affect how people perceive events and others. Once a social schema is activated, it may be difficult to adjust a perception of a person or event.

Stereotypes and Prejudice

Cognitive schemas can result in stereotypes and contribute to prejudice.

Stereotypes

Stereotypes are beliefs about people based on their membership in a particular group. Stereotypes can be positive, negative, or neutral. Stereotypes based on gender, ethnicity, or occupation are common in many societies.

The Stability of Stereotypes

Stereotypes are not easily changed, for the following reasons:

- When people encounter instances that disconfirm their stereotypes of a particular group, they tend to assume that those instances are atypical subtypes of the group.

- People's perceptions are influenced by their expectations.
- People selectively recall instances that confirm their stereotypes and forget about disconfirming instances.

Functions

Stereotypes have several important functions:

- They allow people to quickly process new information about an event or person.
- They organize people's past experiences.
- They help people to meaningfully assess differences between individuals and groups.
- They help people to make predictions about other people's behavior.

Dangers

Stereotypes can lead to distortions of reality for several reasons:

- They cause people to exaggerate differences among groups.
- They lead people to focus selectively on information that agrees with the stereotype and ignore information that disagrees with it.
- They tend to make people see other groups as overly homogenous, even though people can easily see that the groups they belong to are heterogeneous.

Prejudice

A **prejudice** is a negative belief or feeling about a particular group of individuals. Prejudices are often passed on from one generation to the next.

Functions

Prejudice is a destructive phenomenon, and it is pervasive because it serves many psychological, social, and economic functions:

- Prejudice allows people to avoid doubt and fear.
- Prejudice gives people scapegoats to blame in times of trouble.

- Prejudice can boost self-esteem.
- Evolutionary psychologists suggest that prejudice allows people to bond with their own group by contrasting it to outsider groups.
- Prejudice legitimizes discrimination because it apparently justifies one group's dominance over another.

Reducing Prejudice

Research shows that prejudice and conflict among groups can be reduced if four conditions are met:

- The groups have equality in terms of legal status, economic opportunity, and political power.
- Authorities advocate equal rights.
- The groups have opportunities to interact formally and informally with each other.
- The groups cooperate to reach a common goal.

Attitudes

Attitudes are evaluations people make about objects, ideas, events, or other people. Attitudes can be positive or negative. **Explicit attitudes** are conscious beliefs that can guide decisions and behavior. **Implicit attitudes** are unconscious beliefs that can still influence decisions and behavior. Attitudes can include up to three components: cognitive, emotional, and behavioral.

Dimensions of Attitudes

Researchers study three dimensions of attitude: strength, accessibility, and ambivalence.

- **Attitude strength:** Strong attitudes are those that are firmly held and that highly influence behavior. Attitudes that are important to a person tend to be strong. Attitudes that people have a vested interest in also tend to be strong. Furthermore, people tend to have stronger attitudes about things, events, ideas, or people they have considerable knowledge and information about.

- **Attitude accessibility:** The accessibility of an attitude refers to the ease with which it comes to mind. In general, highly accessible attitudes tend to be stronger.
- **Attitude ambivalence:** Ambivalence of an attitude refers to the ratio of positive and negative evaluations that make up that attitude. The ambivalence of an attitude increases as the positive and negative evaluations get more and more equal.

The Influence of Attitudes on Behavior

Behavior does not always reflect attitudes. However, attitudes do determine behavior in some situations:

- If there are few outside influences, attitude guides behavior.
- Behavior is guided by attitudes specific to that behavior.
- Behavior is guided by attitudes that come to mind easily.

The Influence of Behavior on Attitudes

Behavior also affects attitudes. People tend to be more likely to agree to a difficult request if they have first agreed to an easy one. This is called the **foot-in-the door phenomenon**.

Attitude Change

Researchers have proposed three theories to account for attitude change: learning theory, dissonance theory, and the elaboration likelihood model.

Learning Theory

Learning theory says that attitudes can be formed and changed through the use of learning principles such as classical conditioning, operant conditioning, and observational learning:

- **Classical conditioning:** The emotional component of attitudes can be formed through classical conditioning. For example, in a billboard ad, a clothing company pairs a sweater with an attractive model who elicits a pleasant emotional response.
- **Operant conditioning:** If someone gets a positive response from others when she expresses an attitude, that attitude will be reinforced and will tend to get stronger. On the other hand, if she gets a negative response from others, that attitude tends to get weaker.
- **Observational learning:** Seeing others display a particular attitude and watching people be reinforced for expressing a particular attitude can make someone adopt those attitudes.

Dissonance Theory

Leon Festinger's **dissonance theory** proposes that people change their attitudes when they have attitudes that are inconsistent with each other. Festinger said that people experience **cognitive dissonance** when they have related cognitions that conflict with one another. Cognitive dissonance results in a state of unpleasant tension. People try to reduce the tension by changing their attitudes.

The phenomenon called justification of effort also results from cognitive dissonance. Justification of effort refers to the idea that if people work hard to reach a goal, they are likely to value the goal more. They justify working hard by believing that the goal is valuable.

The Elaboration Likelihood Model

The elaboration likelihood model holds that attitude change is more permanent if the elaborate and thought-provoking persuasive messages are used to change the attitude. Basically, if someone can provide a thorough, thought-provoking persuasive message to change an attitude, he is more likely to succeed than if he provides a neutral or shallow persuasive message.

Attraction

Interpersonal attraction refers to positive feelings about another person. It can take many forms, including liking, love, friendship, lust, and admiration.

Influences

Many factors influence attraction. They include physical attractiveness, proximity, similarity, and reciprocity:

- **Physical attractiveness:** Research shows that romantic attraction is primarily determined by physical attractiveness. In the early stages of dating, people are more attracted to partners whom they consider to be physically attractive. Men are more likely to value physical attractiveness than are women. People's perception of their own physical attractiveness also plays a role in romantic love. The **matching hypothesis** proposes that people tend to pick partners who are about equal in level of attractiveness to themselves.

- **Proximity:** People are more likely to become friends with people who are geographically close. One explanation for this is the **mere exposure effect**. The mere exposure effect refers to people's tendency to like novel stimuli more if they encounter them repeatedly.

- **Similarity:** People also tend to pick partners who are similar to themselves in characteristics such as age, race, religion, social class, personality, education, intelligence, and attitude. This similarity is seen not only between romantic partners but also between friends. Some researchers have suggested that similarity causes attraction. Others acknowledge that people may be more likely to have friends and partners who are similar to themselves simply because of accessibility: people are more likely to associate with people who are similar to themselves.

- **Reciprocity:** People tend to like others who reciprocate their liking.

Romantic Love

Many researchers focus on one particular form of attraction: romantic love.

Kinds of Romantic Love

Researchers have proposed that romantic love includes two kinds of love: passionate love and compassionate love. These two kinds of love may occur together, but they do not always go hand in hand in a relationship.

- **Passionate love:** Involves absorption in another person, sexual desire, tenderness, and intense emotion.
- **Compassionate love:** Involves warmth, trust, and tolerance of another person. Compassionate love is sometimes considered to have two components: intimacy and commitment.
- **Intimacy** is the warm, close, sharing aspect of a relationship.
- **Commitment** is the intent to continue the relationship even in the face of difficulties. Researchers believe commitment is a good predictor of the stability of a relationship.

Attachment Styles

Some researchers study the influence of childhood attachment styles on adult relationships. Many researchers believe that as adults, people relate to their partners in the same way that they related to their caretakers in infancy.

Obedience and Authority

Obedience is compliance with commands given by an authority figure. In the 1960s, the social psychologist **Stanley Milgram** did a famous research study called the obedience study. It showed that people have a strong tendency to comply with authority figures.

Milgram's Obedience Study

Milgram told his forty male volunteer research subjects that they were participating in a study about the effects of punishment on learning. He assigned each of the subjects to the role of teacher. Each subject was told that his task was to help another subject like himself learn a list of word pairs. Each time the learner made a mistake, the teacher was to give the learner an electric shock by flipping a switch. The teacher was told to increase the shock level each time the learner made a mistake, until a dangerous shock level was reached.

Throughout the course of the experiment, the experimenter firmly commanded the teachers to follow the instructions they had been given. In reality, the learner was not an experiment subject but Milgram's accomplice, and he never actually received an electric shock. However, he pretended to be in pain when shocks were administered.

Prior to the study, forty psychiatrists that Milgram consulted told him that fewer than 1 percent of subjects would administer what they thought were dangerous shocks to the learner. However, Milgram found that two-thirds of the teachers did administer even the highest level of shock, despite believing that the learner was suffering great pain and distress. Milgram believed that the teachers had acted in this way because they were pressured to do so by an authority figure.

Factors that Increase Obedience

Milgram found that subjects were more likely to obey in some circumstances than others. Obedience was highest when:

- Commands were given by an authority figure rather than another volunteer
- The experiments were done at a prestigious institution
- The authority figure was present in the room with the subject
- The learner was in another room
- The subject did not see other subjects disobeying commands

In everyday situations, people obey orders because they want to get rewards, because they want to avoid the negative consequences of disobeying, and because they believe an authority is legitimate. In more extreme situations, people obey even when they are required to violate their own values or commit crimes. Researchers think several factors cause people to carry obedience to extremes:

- People justify their behavior by assigning responsibility to the authority rather than themselves.
- People define the behavior that's expected of them as routine.
- People don't want to be rude or offend the authority.
- People obey easy commands first and then feel compelled to obey more and more difficult commands. This process is called entrapment, and it illustrates the foot-in-the-door phenomenon.

Groups

Social psychologists consider a **group** to be composed of two or more people who interact and depend on each other in some way. Examples of groups include a baseball team, an Internet listserv, a college psychology class, and a cult.

Features of Groups

Groups usually have the following features:

- Norms that determine appropriate behavior
- Roles that are assigned to people that determine what behaviors and responsibilities people should take on
- A communication structure that determines who talks to whom within the group
- A power structure that determines how much authority and influence group members have

Conformity

Conformity is the process of giving in to real or imagined pressure from a group. In the 1950s, the psychologist **Solomon Asch** did a famous study that demonstrated that people often conform.

Asch's Conformity Study

Asch recruited male undergraduate subjects for the study and told them that he was doing research on visual perception. He placed each subject in a room with six accomplices. The subject thought that the six were also subjects. The seven people were then given a series of easy tasks. In each task, they looked at two cards, one with a single line on it and the other with three lines of different lengths. The people were asked to decide which line on the second card was the same length as the line on the first card. On the first two tasks, the accomplices announced the correct answer to the group, as did the subject. On the next twelve tasks, the accomplices picked a line on the second card that was clearly a wrong answer. When put in this situation, more than one-third of the subjects conformed to the choices made by their group.

Reasons for Conforming

People have many reasons for conforming:

- They want to be accepted by the group, or they fear rejection by the group. In this case, the group is exerting **normative social influence**.
- The group provides them with information. In this case, the group is exerting **informational social influence**.
- They want a material or social reward, such as a pay raise or votes.
- They admire the group and want to be like other group members.

Group Decision Making

Members of a group are often required to make decisions together. Three concepts related to group decision making are groupthink, group polarization, and minority influence.

Groupthink

Groupthink is the tendency for a close-knit group to emphasize consensus at the expense of critical thinking and rational decision making. In a groupthink situation, group members squash dissent, exert pressure to conform, suppress information from outside the group, and focus selectively on information that agrees with the group's point of view.

Groupthink is more likely to occur when groups have certain characteristics:

- High cohesiveness: **Group cohesiveness** is the strength of the liking and commitment group members have toward each other and to the group.
- Isolation from outside influences
- A strong leader
- The intent to reach a major decision

Group Polarization

The dominant point of view in a group often tends to be strengthened to a more extreme position after a group discussion, a phenomenon called **group polarization**. When a group starts out with a dominant view that is relatively risky, the group is likely to come to a consensus that is even riskier. This phenomenon is called **risky shift**.

Minority Influence

A committed minority viewpoint can change the majority opinion in a group. Group members are more likely to be influenced by a minority opinion when the minority holds the opinion firmly.

Helping Behavior

Social psychologists study the circumstances in which people offer help to others.

The Bystander Effect

Research shows that people are less likely to offer help to someone in distress if other people are also present. This is called the **bystander effect**. The probability that a person will receive help decreases as the number of people present increases.

Diffusion of responsibility contributes to the bystander effect. A person does not feel as responsible for helping someone if several others are also present, since responsibility is distributed among all those present.

Influences on Helping

Researchers have proposed that bystanders who witness an emergency will help only if three conditions are met:

- They notice the incident.
- They interpret the incident as being an emergency situation.
- They assume responsibility for helping.

Researchers suggest that people are most likely to help others in certain circumstances:

- They have just seen others offering help.
- They are not in a hurry.
- They share some similarities with the person needing help.
- They are in a small town or a rural setting.
- They feel guilty.
- They are not preoccupied or focused on themselves.
- They are happy.
- The person needing help appears deserving of help.

Reasons for Helping Others

Some social psychologists use the **social exchange theory** to explain why people help others. They argue that people help each other because they want to gain as much as possible while losing as little as possible. The **social responsibility norm** also explains helping behavior. The social responsibility norm is a societal rule that tells people they should help others who need help even if doing so is costly.

Another norm that explains helping behavior is the **reciprocity norm**, which is the implicit societal rule that says people must help those who have helped them.

Summary

Impressions

- People form impressions about others through the process of person perception.
- People's physical appearance strongly influences the way they are perceived by others.
- People are particularly influenced by physical attractiveness and baby-faced features.
- Social schemas affect how people perceive events and other people.

Stereotypes and Prejudice

- Stereotypes are beliefs about people based on their membership in a particular group.
- Stereotypes tend to be difficult to change.
- Stereotyping has some important functions, but it can also distort reality in dangerous ways.
- A prejudice is a negative belief or feeling about a particular group of individuals.
- Prejudice is pervasive because it serves many social and psychological functions.
- Research shows that there are effective ways to reduce prejudice.

Attitudes

- Attitudes are evaluations people make about objects, ideas, events, or other people. They can be explicit or implicit and can include beliefs, emotions, and behavior.
- Attitudes vary according to strength, accessibility, and ambivalence.
- Attitudes do not always affect behavior.
- The foot-in-the-door phenomenon and the prison study show that behavior can affect attitudes.

- Theories that account for attitude change are learning theory, dissonance theory, and the elaboration likelihood model.

Attraction

- Interpersonal attraction refers to positive feelings about another person.
- Physical attractiveness, proximity, similarity, and reciprocity influence attraction.
- Romantic love includes passionate and compassionate love.
- Compassionate love includes intimacy and commitment.
- Infant attachment styles tend to be reproduced in adult relationships.

Obedience and Authority

- Obedience is compliance with commands given by an authority figure.
- Stanley Milgram's obedience study showed that people have a strong tendency to comply with authority figures.
- The degree of obedience depends on many situational factors.
- People sometimes carry obedience to extremes.

Groups

- A group is a social unit composed of two or more people who interact and depend on each other in some way.
- Groups tend to have distinct norms, roles, communication structures, and power structures.
- Conformity is the process of giving in to real or imagined pressure from a group.
- Solomon Asch did a famous study that showed that people often conform and that social roles influence behavior.
- People conform because of normative social influence, because of informational social influence, because they want to gain rewards, and because they identify with the group.

- Groupthink, group polarization, and minority influence affect decision-making in groups.

Helping Behavior

- People are less likely to offer help in the presence of other people.
- Bystanders are more likely to help people in some circumstances than others.
- Explanations for helping behavior include social exchange theory, the social responsibility norm, and the reciprocity norm.